Cambridge Monographs and Texts in Applied Psycholinguistics

The units of language acquisition

Cambridge Monographs and Texts in Applied Psycholinguistics

General Editor: Sheldon Rosenberg

The units of language acquisition

ANN M. PETERS

University of Hawaii

CAMBRIDGE UNIVERSITY PRESS

Cambridge
London   New York   New Rochelle
Melbourne   Sydney

Published by the Press Syndicate of the University of Cambridge
The Pitt Building, Trumpington Street, Cambridge CB2 1RP
32 East 57th Street, New York, NY 10022, USA
296 Beaconsfield Parade, Middle Park, Melbourne 3206, Australia

First published 1983

Printed in the United States of America

Library of Congress Cataloging in Publication Data
Peters, Ann M., 1938–
The units of language acquisition.
(Cambridge monographs and texts in applied psycholinguistics)
Includes index.
1. Language acquisition. I. Title. II. Series.
P118.P43 1983   401.'9   82–22161
ISBN 0-521-27071-5 hard covers
ISBN 0-521-25810-3 paperback

Contents

Series preface

Ann Peters's *The units of language acquisition* inaugurates a new series for researchers, practitioners, instructors, and students: Cambridge Monographs and Texts in Applied Psycholinguistics. The aim of the series is to draw together work from all the subfields of applied psycholinguistics by authors who approach applied problems from the vantage point of basic research and theory in related areas of cognitive psychology as well as psycholinguistics. It will encompass a wide range of books: reports of original research; critical integrative reviews; major theoretical contributions; presentations of intervention programs for the language-disordered; language assessment programs; carefully selected and edited collections of research and other papers including, possibly, occasional conference reports and symposia; and, an important series component, texts.

The main topics of interest are: reading and reading disorders; writing and writing disorders; learning from texts and lectures; second-language learning and bilingualism; dialect and social-class differences; the assessment of linguistic maturity and communicative competence; the application of psycholinguistics to computer language design and the design of written and oral information; nonverbal communication; delayed language development; adult aphasia; autistic language; adult schizophrenic language; and language and communicative disorders associated with mental retardation, environmental deprivation, motor impairment, specific learning disabilities, deafness, blindness, or senile dementia.

Sheldon Rosenberg

Preface

The investigation that led to the writing of this book began when I realized that the language development of a child I was studying was not progressing in any previously documented manner. By beginning to observe this child, Minh, at the age of 7 months, I had planned to trace the transition from babbling to speech, and ultimately to connect my observations on his one-word stage with the growing literature on early learning of syntax. What I discovered, however, was that while he was learning a number of traditional "words" (*doggie, kitty, cookie,* etc.), Minh's speech consisted more characteristically of relatively long sentencelike utterances, only some of which could be identified with adult words or phrases (*look at that! what is that? open the door!*). Thus notions such as "word" and "syntax" were called into serious question when applied to his language acquisition. This and other problems led me to question many of the traditional models and assumptions about early language acquisition and to propose, in Peters (1977), that there might be a "Gestalt," in addition to the more familiar "Analytic," approach to acquiring language.

In searching the literature on the one-word stage I discovered a number of hints suggesting that Minh was not the only child to use a Gestalt strategy – or more accurately to combine a Gestalt with an Analytic approach. Although the material that I had found up to that time was incorporated into the 1977 paper, I was not satisfied. There was still the question: Is the Gestalt approach some kind of anomaly, a false lead that eventually peters out in a dead end? Or is it an important and pervasive strategy, but one that has been missed owing to theoretical biases of child language investigators? As I continued to read I steadily accumulated reports of observations that support the latter view, although, it seems, no author has attempted to integrate it into a reasonably comprehensive theory of language acquisition.

I gradually discovered that the key to the integration was that, whether a Gestalt or an Analytic approach was used, children must in general start out with whatever units they can acquire, whether large or small. Therefore, to understand early language acquisition, one must understand the language units that children are actually working with. There is no reason to assume that these are necessarily the same as the units of adult language. I set myself two tasks, the pursuit of which has resulted in this book. One goal was to formulate this view as clearly as possible and to integrate it with a wide range of reported research on language acquisition. The task proved surprisingly difficult since the ideas were so new and the relevant published observations were reported in such a tortuous fashion, reflecting the lack of appropriate terminology and conceptual framework. The other goal was to understand the implications of this model clearly enough so that I could devise specific research methods for investigating particular aspects of the phenomena that I was proposing were common to all children. Thus, although in this account suggestions for further research are mostly confined to Chapter 5, they must be seen as a major contribution of the work.

This book is a much revised and expanded version of an earlier working paper (Peters 1980). As the ideas presented here are better understood and further developed, it should be possible to reformulate them in clearer and more succinct ways. Although I am convinced of the validity of the overall approach, particular aspects of the theory may need revision in the light of the results of the proposed new research.

I have drawn on the ideas and observations of a large number of child language and even adult language investigators. It has not been possible to acknowledge accurately all the possible sources of each idea that I have mentioned or developed, although the range of my debt to them is accurately reflected in the References section at the end of the book. In addition, I would like to single out certain of the principal influences on my work. My conviction that children's language units are central to a theory of the early stages of language acquisition was greatly influenced by the work of Ruth Clark and Katherine Nelson. A preliminary paper I had formulated by the spring of 1979 was strongly reinforced by interactions with Charles Fillmore and Lily Wong Fillmore that summer. More recent versions of the theory were influenced by my exposure to Dan Slobin's cross-linguistic work on language acquisition in the summer of 1980, as well as by the latest version of his Operating Principles, to which I was introduced in his seminar at Berkeley in the winter of 1981. To Shirley Brice Heath I am grateful for the chance to discuss ideas about cross-cultural influences on the size of linguistic units. Other colleagues whom I thank for discussions and comments are Carol Tane Akamatsu, Elizabeth Barber, Ruth Berman, John Bisazza, Stephen Boggs, Eileen Cain, Bonnie Davis, Susan Fischer, Joan Forman, George Grace, Robert Hsu, A. W. F. Huggins, Susan Iwamura, Elizabeth Kimmell, Stephen Krashen, Anita Nordbrock, Claudine Poggi, Jack Richards, Theodore Rodgers, Robin Scarcella, Jacquelyn Schachter, Ron Scollon, Stanley Starosta, Harry Whitaker, and the participants in Dan Slobin's seminar at the

University of California at Berkeley during the winter quarter of 1981. I am also indebted to Sheldon Rosenberg, the editor of this series, and to his consultant, for their perceptive and helpful comments. I wish to thank the Social Science Research Institute of the University of Hawaii for support while I was working on this project. The text owes much of its present shape to the constant encouragement and merciless editing of my friend and colleague Robert W. Hsu. I alone am responsible for the content.

Ann M. Peters

Conventions

The following conventions are used in my own examples and discussion, though not necessarily in examples quoted from others:

Material in double quotation marks: either a technical term or what someone else actually said – a direct quotation, for example, "I don't wanna."

Material in single quotation marks: a gloss of what someone said – either a translation from another language or an interpretation of child speech, for example, 'look at that'.

Material in italics: emphasis; phonological stress (in quoted speech); or the target of an utterance, that is, a word or phrase being aimed at, for example, *look at that*.

Underscored materials in italics: Underlines show presumed lack of segmentation, for example, *I don't know what that is*.

Material in square brackets: phonetic transcription, for example, [dʊkədæt].

Material between slashes: phonemic transcription, for example, /heyv/.

Children's ages are given as: years;months.days, for example, 2;3.12.

1   Units of speech

Child language researchers have generally approached the description of first-language acquisition using the traditional apparatus of adult language description. They have, for instance, focused on the emergence of adult words, on the development of adult morphological processes, on the classification of "one-word utterances" as opposed to "two-word constructions," and on the emergence of adultlike syntactic structures.[1] On the other hand, they have specifically ignored the vast quantity of early utterances (the entire early output of some children at some stages) in which such units and constructions cannot be readily distinguished (see discussion in Scollon 1976, 24–36). They have also failed to study the processes leading up to the emergence of recognizable words.

It is, however, in the very residue of heretofore ignored utterances that we find clues to these processes. This book presents a new view of these processes, marshaling the evidence for their existence, showing how variability among children's early speech productions can be easily understood in relation to these processes, and pointing to further research possibilities growing out of this view.

I will first need to sketch three distinct orientations to the seemingly intuitive notion of "minimal unit of speech." The first concerns the unit of speech production used by the adult speaker. The second concerns the first-language learner's perception of appropriate units in an unknown language and her or his attempts to produce them. The third concerns the child language investigator's efforts to identify and describe the units that the child has perceived and uses. Inadequate awareness of these distinct orientations, coupled with the linguist's overriding concern with economy of description, has obscured what the data of early language acquisition are trying to tell us.

---

[1] A few examples of such studies, representative of the work on early stages of language acquisition, are, for vocabulary development, Leopold (1939), Nelson (1973); for morphological development, Berko (1958), Brown (1973); for single- vs. multi-word utterances, Bloom (1973), Scollon (1976); for syntactic development, Bloom (1970), Brown, Cazden, & Bellugi (1969).

1

1.1.   Units from the adult's point of view

Relatively little linguistic research has been done to identify the actual units from which mature speakers construct utterances. The focus has rather been on describing only the corpus of utterances themselves (the "language") in the most economical and nonredundant terms, regardless of how they were produced. Descriptions of adult, and in fact also child, language therefore strive to minimize both the number and size of the basic distinctive units used. Thus one looks for distinctive features in phonology, and morphemes in syntax, rather than functional units as measured, for instance, by occurrence of invariant combinations, fluency of production, or characteristic intonation contours (see 1.3 for further discussion).

If this model of language is taken also as an accurate model of the adult speaker, it implies that the speaker stores the lexicon and grammar in the most nonredundant form and produces each utterance afresh from the minimal units. Evidence has been accumulating, however, that normal adult speakers actually store and call into play entire phrases that may be many words long – phrases that are not constructed from their ultimate grammatical constituents each time they are used. Accordingly, while words and morphemes may be the ultimate units in a logical and economical description of a *language*, the actual units used in *speech production* may be different (see, e.g., Bisazza 1978; Bolinger 1975; Hayes-Roth 1977; Pawley & Syder 1976; Wong Fillmore 1976). I will now examine the nature of these larger units.

In what follows I will use the term "speech formula" to mean a multimorphemic phrase or sentence that, either through social negotiation or through individual evolution, has become available to a speaker as a single prefabricated item in her or his lexicon. Not only are such formulas fixed in structure; they also tend to be rather strongly situationally conditioned. They range from memorized sequences (such as counting, the alphabet, nursery rhymes), through swear phrases *(goddammit)*, exclamations *(oh boy)*, greeting and leave-taking rituals *(how are you, see you)*, social control phrases *(lookit, my turn, shut up)*, to idioms *(kick the bucket)* and small talk *(isn't it a lovely day)* (see Wong Fillmore 1976 for a more complete discussion, and also Ferguson 1976 on politeness formulas and Fraser 1970 on idioms).

In fact, the range of formulaic speech is probably even greater than this, extending into the realms of jargon, technical language, and intimate speech: all those areas in which expressions can be negotiated among a small number of parties until they achieve very specific meanings known only to the parties involved. Nagy demonstrates the existence in English of certain phrases that, although grammatically analyzable and therefore not idiomatic, are nonetheless restricted in their combinatorial privileges to the extent that they and their components must be separately specified in the lexicon. He describes these phrases as "semi-productive" and sees them as constituting "a significant area where sentences are constructed out of prefabricated chunks rather than being built from scratch on the spot" (1978, 289). Pawley and Syder (1976) take an extreme position on the extent of formulaic speech available to the speaker, claiming that in order to achieve "native-like fluency" in ordinary conversation the speaker must make extensive, if not almost exclusive, use of what they call "institutionalized clauses." In general such clauses are not idioms, in that they are analyzable by ("transparent" to) the grammar of the language (as idioms are not), but for efficiency of processing they are nevertheless stored whole and not generated from scratch each time they are needed.

We may further need to recognize the continuum between "cultural formulas," which, judging from their invariance in form, are treated as units in a particular speech community (whether of two or a million persons), and "idiosyncratic formulas," which may have a prefabricated status only for one particular speaker (for further discussion see 4.2.1). Thus, if I find an especially felicitous way of expressing an idea, I may store up that turn of phrase so that the next time I need it it will come forth as a prefabricated chunk, even though to my hearer it may not be distinguishable from newly generated speech. This last kind of expression, then, not only is completely analyzable by the grammar of the language but as a result of its transparency has a dual status for the speaker: It can be handled either as a single unit or as a complex construction with internal structure (e.g., words can be inserted into or deleted from the phrase, or the grammatical structure can be changed as needed). Bateson suggests the useful term "praxon" for chunks of speech or other behavior that, "regardless of internal structure, are either used or interpreted as unitary" (1975, 61).

For mature speakers of a language, then, formulaic speech may serve as a shortcutting device: It saves processing time and effort, allowing the speaker to focus attention elsewhere, for instance, on the social (as opposed to the linguistic) aspects of an interaction, or, as Pawley and Syder suggest, on the macrostructure of a discourse rather than on the generation of individual sentences. The idea that speakers indeed make use of such shortcutting devices as knowledge becomes consolidated is consistent with the "knowledge assembly theory" proposed by Hayes-Roth, who postulates a process of "unitization" that creates an "assembly" of smaller units of knowledge ("cogits"). Such a unitized assembly is then always "activated in an all-or-none fashion" (1977, 261). Bisazza goes so far as to propose that each adult speaker of a language has constructed a whole continuum of grammars, each of which "is capable of serving as a template for linguistic behavior" (Claim 2); that this continuum "can be characterized on the basis of principles of relatively more or less differentiation and abstract analysis and systematization" (Claim 3); and that "the adult's choice of TL [Templating

Level] for a particular instance of performance is determined by a kind of least effort principle: the [simplest] TL capable of correctly templating the encoding or decoding behavior in a given context is usually chosen" (Claim 6) (1978, 78–9). Such a suggestion implies that, far from employing a minimal amount of storage space for our language, we keep on hand many representations of the "same" information, choosing in any given instance exactly that one which minimizes processing effort.

Another important aspect of some speech formulas is that they may not be entirely fixed, but may be only partly set, having one or more open "slots" that can be filled in with grammatically appropriate words according to the speaker's needs, for example, *how are you* + time phrase *(today, this morning,* etc.). I will call such constructions "formulaic frames with analyzed slots," after Wong Fillmore (1979). Krashen and Scarcella use the term "prefabricated patterns" to refer to constructions that are "partly 'creative' and partly memorized wholes," and the term "prefabricated routines" for "memorized whole utterances or phrases," that is, what I call "speech formulas" (1978, 283).

A last point that I wish to clarify about formulaic speech is its relationship to what has been called "automatic speech." The latter term has been used to refer to the speech of brain-damaged patients who, although they have little or no productive control of propositional (creative) speech, are nevertheless able to utter certain stereotypical words or phrases (see van Lancker 1975, 110–47, for a full discussion). Although such utterances share with formulaic speech the property of being fixed in form, they differ in that for any given patient the available repertory of such utterances is extremely limited and there is no creative aspect to them at all. It is an intriguing question how these utterances can remain available to patients when propositional speech is destroyed – perhaps through strong emotional associations or some sort of overlearning. Furthermore, as Huebner (1982, 40) points out, the automatic speech of aphasics tends to be used without regard to appropriateness, whereas language learners always attempt to use their formulaic speech in socially and linguistically appropriate ways. Suffice it to say that "formulaic speech" is not here to be taken as synonymous with "automatic speech"; rather, the latter is seen as at most a very limited subset of the former. This point is relevant because Krashen and Scarcella use the terms "automatic speech" and "routines" (which I here call "formulas") as if they were synonymous (1978, 286–9), placing both in opposition to creative speech. I propose in this book, however, that formulaic speech, but not automatic speech, is merely a facet of creative language.

1.2. Units from the child's point of view

The recognition of the ubiquity of formulas in speech production is central to our inquiry into child language acquisition in several ways. First, it focuses our attention on the nature of the raw data with which the child has to work. It is not a dictionary of morphemes that the child is exposed to, but rather an intermittent stream of speech sounds containing chunks, often longer than a single word, that recur with varying frequency. It is out of this stream of unknown meaning and structure that the child must attempt to capture some pieces in order to determine their meaning and to preserve them for future use.

To some extent the child's problem is not unlike that of a cryptographer who, faced with an undeciphered text that has no markings for word or sentence breaks, must determine where meaningful divisions occur (Barber 1974, 14). The child's problem is more difficult in that it must be solved in real time: There is no possibility of going back and rereading the text. When considered in this cryptographic light it is not surprising that missegmentation errors should occur; what is surprising is that so little should have been written about this process, and that it has not become a focus of systematic investigation. Tangential treatments can be found in Brown (1973), Clark (1974, 1977), MacWhinney (1974), and Wong Fillmore (1976).

Secondly, awareness of formulas alerts us to the possibility that when we hear a child produce an utterance containing several words of the adult language, it may consist of only one "unit" for the child, just as the adult utterance(s) after which it was modeled may have been produced as single formulas.

It has in fact been noted in the literature that the speech of certain children often contains formulaic phrases that the child could not have constructed from their constituents. For instance, in commenting on Bloom's observations of children's ability to remember and reproduce complex linguistic material, Olson says, "Such utterances manifest structures that are nonproductive in the child's language at that particular stage, but the utterances are used as a unit for some specific semantic or pragmatic purpose without the child's knowing in some sense the internal structure of the string" (1973, 156). I propose in this book that this phenomenon is a manifestation of one of the central processes in all early language acquisition. This process is the extraction of pieces, or "units," from the speech stream in which the child is immersed. Since the child does not know the language, it is unreasonable to assume that the first units she or he extracts will coincide exactly with the words and morphemes of the system. On the other hand, it *is* reasonable to assume that at the earliest stages there is a cognitive limitation constraining the child to processing (e.g., extracting and producing) what to the child is one unit at a time. For production, at least, it has been implicitly assumed that this limitation exists. Certainly the existence of a "one-word stage" of language acquisition is accepted without question by researchers in the field (see, e.g., the summaries in Clark & Clark 1977, 300–304; Dale 1976, 8–17, deVilliers &

deVilliers 1978, 48–52). This stage would, however, have been more accurately labeled the "one-unit stage."[2]

Finally, recognizing that children may be extracting phrases as well as words as their first units can explain the wide range of variation in the size of these units, measured in conventional words or morphemes (or even syllables).[3] Thus one child's early vocabulary may consist primarily of one-word labels (e.g., Halliday's Nigel [1975, 148–54]; Scollon's Brenda [1976, 47]; Nelson's Jane, Paul, Leslie, and Ellen [1973, 104, 106, 109, 110]), whereas another's may contain a higher proportion of multimorphemic expressions (e.g., Nelson's Lisa [107], Mark [111], Robert [112]; Peters's Minh [1977, 563–7]). I shall return to this variability in the next chapter.

1.3. Units from the linguist's point of view

A linguist typically has motives for recognizing units different from those a child or adult speaker has. The linguists' bias of looking for words and morphemes has probably contributed to their overlooking the fact that the earliest units the child uses are not simply words but units of another kind. Some of these units happen to coincide with words of the adult language, a matter that leads the linguist, trained in a descriptive framework that takes these as minimal units of grammar, to concentrate on these utterances and to ignore the others. Even if a linguist should notice, or wonder about, these residual utterances, however, it is still difficult to accord them serious attention because of two types of factors, one practical and the other more theoretical.

---

[2] I have been unable to find a completely satisfactory term to use for these early productions that, although unitary for the child, are not necessarily so from the standpoint of linguistic analysis. Thus "holophrase," which on the face of it could easily mean "a single unit in the child's linguistic system made up of one or more morphemes of the adult language," is commonly used to mean "a single word used as if it meant a whole sentence." I feel I must also reject Bateson's term "praxon," which is broader in scope and includes units of behavior as well as of language. MacWhinney's term "amalgam," which refers to morphemic combinations (such as *ships*) "formed" by rote memorization (1974, 76), has the right meaning, but seems to have the wrong focus: Rather than pointing up the unitary nature of these early units, it reflects the adult linguist's bias that they really consist of more than one morpheme. I have therefore settled on the less colorful term "unit," which at least implies no more than what is intended.

[3] Notice that the evidence has not shown that at the one-unit stage these units are limited to one *syllable* each. Such a constraint would, of course, limit a child to single words or parts of words. But a quick scan of early vocabulary lists will show many entries such as *mommy, daddy, doggie, kitty, allgone, goodnight*. If a child can process a two-syllable word, she or he should process a two-syllable phrase in the same way – and, in fact, how is the child to distinguish the two, at least at the earliest stages of acquiring the language system?

1.3.1. Identifying the units

Practical factors affecting the linguist's attention to the units the child produces involve the difficulty of inferring the units' actual status – unitary or complex – in the child's system: One must use what the child *produces* to infer what the child currently *perceives* the language system to be. One reason for this problem is that, at the one-unit stage, the child is typically having difficulty controlling the phonology, and the early utterances are so garbled or reduced that it is extremely difficult for the linguist to determine their targets. They in fact do not appear to be suitable material for (traditional) linguistic analysis at all. If it were easier to recognize the multimorphemic nature of some targets we might have had our noses rubbed in the problem; as it is, we have been content with relegating such utterances to the "unintelligible utterance" trash heap. Also, the child's lack of phonological control has as a consequence the fact that there is a wide phonetic variation in the pronunciation of the "same" target from one time to the next (see, e.g., Scollon 1976, 44–5). And when a child is using a "Gestalt" production strategy (see 2.2.1; Peters 1977; Macken 1979), the linguist's difficulty in determining whether or not two utterances are aiming at the same longish target is compounded. (In the case of older children learning a second language, however, phonological control will have developed to the place where, although there may be an accent, the problem of determining initial targets will be much easier; see, e.g., Wong Fillmore 1976).

In the face of these difficulties, how is the linguist to determine what for a particular child is a single unit rather than a multi-unit construction synthesized by the child? Nelson raises this question (1973, 24–5) but concludes that the problem is intractable and decides to retain the adult definition of a word as her unit of analysis. Similarly, although Brown says, "It seems likely to me that in Stage I there are a great many unanalyzed 'chunks' as well as much that is produced by grammatical rules," he does not really pursue the problem further, noting only that "spontaneous speech alone does not enable us to decide in every case which is which" (1973, 212). At the end of his book he does take some space to deal with "the problem of segmentation" (390–8). In considering whether Adam's "it's" and "that-a" are "single morphemes" (i.e., units) for the child, he uses the following criteria: (1) Were the parts ever produced separately? (2) Was the usage of the form overgeneralized in "inappropriate" ways (e.g., "It's fell")? (3) Did overgeneralization *fail* to occur in certain contexts (e.g., *"I want that-a book")? (4) In the speech of the child's parents were the models "usually *not* marked by any manifestation of open junction"? (5) Were they high in frequency in parental speech? I believe that these criteria deserve more attention than Brown himself gave them. They are incorporated in the general set of criteria that I develop shortly.

As long as the child seems to be in the one-unit stage, that is, as long as there seems to be an upper bound of one item (however long in adult syllables or morphemes) on her or his production capacity, we feel on relatively safe ground (e.g., Minh at 14 months producing *uh-oh, look at that, oopsidaisy, what's that? open the door* [Peters 1977, 563–65]). We must, of course, be ready to tell when the child is starting to construct utterances of more than one unit. What methods can we use to distinguish one-unit from multi-unit utterances? Although it may not be possible to make such a decision for every utterance, the following criteria can give us some clues.

1.   Is the utterance an idiosyncratic chunk that the child uses repeatedly and in exactly the same form?

The use of this criterion is illustrated in Clark's description of the speech of her son, Adam:

The fact that copied utterances were retained intact for several weeks without other lexical items being substituted suggests that such utterances also functioned as units with limited internal structure . . . Here is an example:

(9) *Wait for it to cool.*   (Said whenever a hot meal was brought on
                                            to the table.)

Only after several weeks was another adjective substituted for *cool* in the structure yielding:

(10) *Wait for it to dry.*   (Hanging up on a towel rail a nappy that
                                            he'd dropped in the bath.)   [1974, 4]

Similarly, Burling, in his report of his diary study of his son Stephen's acquisition of Garo and English between 1;4 and 2;10, finds the criterion of nonsubstitutability a useful one in determining whether Stephen's productions were unitary or not:

At one year and seven months, I began to notice a few utterances which, from an adult point of view consisted of more than one morpheme. At 1:10 . . . I . . . recorded different inflectional forms of the Garo first person singular pronoun . . . though presumably he learned these individually and did not construct them himself. His closest approach to substitutability was in phrases with the word *ba-o* 'where' as in *po bao* 'where's Paul?'. I heard this word used once or twice with nouns other than 'Paul,' but was still doubtful that these phrases were formed by him. It seemed more likely that all were learned as entire phrases. His speech could thus not be described as having utterances of more than one morpheme, since the constituents were not substitutable. [1973, 80]

2.   Is the construction of the utterance unrelated to any productive pattern in the child's current speech?

This criterion, too, is used by Clark. She asserts that Adam's expression *I could easily do that* at 3;11.2 "was clearly copied as a complete routine from other children at the nursery in competitive situations," and that this was the only expression for a long time in which he ever used *could* (1977, 350).

This criterion is also seen in Bloom: Her lists of Kathryn's and Eric's utterances for which her grammars could not account include "structures that were not productive in that they occurred only once and appeared to be unanalyzed 'stereotype' sentences" (1970,75).

Wong Fillmore also seems to use this criterion in her study of five 5- to 7-year-old second-language learners learning English in a school setting:

> In Nora's spontaneous speech samples at Time I, for example, one finds sentences such as "I don't wanna play wi' dese one" and "I don't know" among others such as "Dese one no want play," "You no do dese" and "She's not give it the money him" . . . In Nora's case, the well-formed negatives were acquired and used as ready-made wholes, while the others apparently were the result of her own efforts at negation.
>
> [1976, 287]

Similarly, MacWhinney notes that "the morphophonological structure of rote forms is often far in advance of the morpophonological structure of productive forms" (1978, 11).

3. Is the utterance somewhat inappropriate in some of the contexts in which it is used?

Clark uses this clue to determine that certain of Adam's utterances were not completely analyzed:

> There were certain utterances which Adam produced which were quite clearly copied as incompletely analysed units, and given only a global interpretation with reference to the situation. For example,

(7) *Sit my knee.*	(Used when the child wanted to sit on an adult's knee, and probably copied from an adult saying "Sit on my knee.")
(8) *I carry you.*	(Said when the child wanted to be carried and definitely copied in the first instance from his father, who said "I'll carry you.")

> The child's strategy here seemed to be to copy the utterance produced by the adult and use it himself in similar situations, without making any modifications for the new speaker.
>
> In the above examples the fact that the child had not fully accommodated to the syntax of the utterances he had copied was evident from the way he misapplied them. [1974, 3–4]

Similarly van der Geest gives some examples where his son, Mark, who was learning Dutch, evidently copied whole expressions without adjusting the pronouns:

Around age 2;2 he could be expected to say such things as

(11)   *Jij doet dat* (You do that); meaning: "I do that."
(12)   *Is dat van jou?* (Is that yours); meaning: "Is that mine?"   [1977, 98]

4.   Does the utterance cohere phonologically?

That is, is it always produced fluently as a unit with an unbroken intonation contour and no hesitations for encoding? Note that whereas for adults hesitation pauses are not reliable indicators of the size and nature of encoding units (Rosenberg 1977), the dual criteria of presence versus absence of hesitation and double versus single intonation contour have been fairly widely used in child language research to distinguish a succession of two one-word utterances from a single two-word construction. Thus Scollon uses these criteria to separate "vertical" from "horizontal" constructions (1976, 152–3). Branigan and Stokes, too, on the basis of their phonetic analysis of the prosodic integration of early utterances, propose two classes of utterances: those that are temporally fragmented (with pauses) and those that are temporally unified (1981, 8). It would seem, therefore, that at least for very young children the absence of pauses together with the presence of smooth intonation contours is a good clue to some kind of preplanned psycholinguistic unit. And a particular sequence of adult morphemes that is always marked by such phonological coherence (i.e., one in which there are never any hesitations in the middle) is a good candidate for a unit in the child's system.

Certain early utterances may even have special intonation contours associated with them. Minh as early as 1;2 had easily recognizable "tunes" for the expressions *what's that? look at that!* and *uh-oh!* (Peters 1977). These utterances were also marked by phonological integration: They were articulated as units, the most common forms being ['ʌsǽ:], [dùkədǽ:], and ['ɔ́'ɔ:].

Wong Fillmore suggests another criterion (1976, 310):

5.   Is the usage of the expression situationally dependent for the child?

The fact that a particular expression always occurs in a particular well-defined context may be a clue to the linguist that this expression is an unanalyzed part of a set routine with which the child has become familiar through frequent repetition. Daily or otherwise regular activities in the child's life, such as greeting the family in the morning, mealtime rituals, greeting Daddy when he returns from work, or leaving the family to go to bed, can provide the child with regular "scripts," complete in setting, dialogue, and accompanying activities, which the child can come to know, anticipate, and eventually participate in. In 2.2.2 and 3.4.3 I will discuss at more length the potential importance of such routines in the process of language learning; here my focus is on the heuristic value to the linguist of such predictable contexts in identifying potential speech units.

An example of such a contextually defined early unit can be found in my data from Minh. At 14 months he produced a series of utterances, roughly, ['òbɛdədɛ́]. From his actions – he was pounding on a closed door and shouting to his older brother on the other side – it is clear that what he was saying was 'open the door.' From other evidence about the stage of his language development it is clear that he was still at the one-unit stage (Peters 1977). Hence we cannot but conclude that *open the door* was a unit for him. A similar contextual dependence (along with evidence of lack of analysis) can be seen in Clark's two examples (just quoted): *sit my knee* and *I carry you.*

Another criterion suggested by Wong Fillmore (1976, 310) is

6. Is the expression a community-wide formula?

Within a given community certain phrases always occur in exactly the same form. Greeting and leave-taking formulas are particularly notable in this regard, for example, *good morning, how are you.* This invariance makes these phrases more likely to be perceived as units and concomitantly less susceptible to analysis. (In fact, even for adults they may become more and more unitary over time. Thus *how do you do* evolved into *howdy* as it became progressively more condensed [Bolinger 1975, 100].) On the other hand, such formulas occur often enough and predictably enough so that they are easily picked up by children and associated with the proper contexts. Children may even be coached in their appropriate use as part of a linguistic socialization process (Gleason & Weintraub 1978). Already at 1;2, Minh could say *thank you*: Although in my data this was articulated once as [təköt] and once as [kyɛ], it is clear what his intended target was because these utterances occurred in a context of giving and receiving.

An example of a child's unitary perception of another kind of community formula comes from Wong Fillmore. In this instance the community in question was the school and the formulaic phrase was *it's recess.* Her subject, 7-year-old Jesus, always condensed this to "s'briseh" (1976, 313). Note that although Wong Fillmore was dealing with older children learning a second language, she, too, was faced with the problem of "one unit or several?"

Even though these heuristics for identifying actual speech units will no doubt be added to and refined, they already provide substantial evidence that it should be possible for the linguist to determine at least some of the child's speech units.

The difficulty of making this determination should no longer be a serious impediment to considering the child's units rather than the adult grammarian's in describing the child's language.

1.3.2.   The place of the units in theory

In addition to the difficulty of ascertaining what are in fact the child's units, another factor that has led linguists to overlook or reject such units has been the lack of a place for them in any existing model of learning or of language. In particular, the units that happen not to coincide with adult words are not used by the rules that the child is presumed to be trying to learn, and they apparently have no other use in language learning. Here I discuss the mismatch between such units and the linguist's expectations.

The assumption of most linguists studying the acquisition of syntax has been that the process moves from little utterances to bigger ones, in both length and complexity. Since the goal of such research is to discover when and how children learn to construct novel utterances of their own, the focus has been on buildup processes, starting with the smallest possible units. Brown describes the problem that the child first faces as follows: "In order to learn grammar, a child must segment the speech he hears into morphemes because morphemes are the ultimate units of grammatical rules" (1973, 390). The potential importance of longer units has been overlooked or dismissed. Thus Leopold justifies disregarding "early complete sentences like *I see you* because they were learned by mechanical phonetic imitation as units. The use of such stereotype phrases has nothing to do with the child's learning to put words together in an original sentence" (1971, 140).

In fact, the learning of such a "stereotype" or "formulaic" phrase as an unanalyzed whole has been seen as an impediment to its speedy analysis in terms of the child's growing productive system. Brown and Hanlon observed that

the parents of Adam, Eve, and Sarah [produced] certain *wh* questions at a very high rate in a period when the children did not understand the structure of *wh* questions . . . The children learned to produce the two most frequently repeated *wh* questions, *What's that?* and *What doing?*, on roughly appropriate occasions. Their performance had the kind of rigidity that we have learned to recognize as a sign of incomprehension of structure: they did not produce, as their parents of course did, such structurally close variants as *What are those?* and *Who's that?* and *What is he doing?* When, much later, the children began to produce all manner of *wh* questions in the preposed form (such as *What he wants*) it was interesting to note that *What's that?* and *What are you doing?* were not at first reconstrued in terms of the new analysis. If the children had generated the sentences in terms of their new rules they ought to have said *What that is?* and *What you are doing?* but instead they, at first, persisted with the old forms . . .

We suggest that any form that is produced with very high frequency by parents will be somehow represented in the child's performance even if its structure is far beyond him.

He will find a way to render a version of it and will also form a notion of the circumstances in which it is used. The construction [*sic*] will become lodged in his speech as an unassimilated fragment. Extensive use of such an unanalyzed or mistakenly analyzed fragment probably protects it, for a time, from reanalysis when the structure relevant to it is finally learned. [1970, 51]

If the memorization of such chunks of "complex linguistic material" does not feed into the process of learning grammar, is it, then, a complete dead end? Or is it perhaps possible that in our preoccupation with discovering adult grammar in the child's language we have failed to observe what happens to such material as the child's linguistic competence grows? Wong Fillmore's monumental study (1976) of five Spanish-speaking children (ages 5 to 7) acquiring English as their second language over nine months provides a model of how a linguist can observe longitudinally the place of certain kinds of speech formulas in children's evolving grammars. It also presents abundant evidence that, at least in this second-language situation, socially relevant formulaic speech was *not* a dead end, but led, through a documentable process of formulaic breakdown, first to formulaic frames with slots and eventually toward analysis into the conventional lexical items and syntactic patterns of the language.

Since 5- to 7-year-old children are not only cognitively more mature than children learning their first language, but also have increased social needs, they may be more prone to memorize long socially appropriate chunks of speech in order to maximize communication with a minimum of language. This difference has been noted by Hatch (1972, 33) and Hakuta (1974, 288), who worked respectively with a 4-year-old and a 5-year-old second-language learner, as well as by Wong Fillmore (1979, 211–12). In the next chapter, however, we will see some evidence that even first-language learners' memories may not be so limited as has been supposed. In any case, Wong Fillmore's work provides a model for a possible analysis of first-language learning, even though such an investigation will have to deal with the handicaps introduced by the less mature child who has poorer phonological control.

There are already hints in the literature that it is possible to observe formulaic breakdown actually occurring in first-language acquisition. Such a hint is found in Burling's report of his son Stephen's acquisition of Garo and English between 1;4 and 2;10. Stephen's approach to language seems to have been very much one of formulaic breakdown. Burling says:

I could readily observe the gradual acquisition of new grammatical constructions and repeatedly the same pattern was followed. He would first learn a number of examples of the construction by rote and at this stage it was generally difficult to tell whether he understood the meaning of the construction or not, though for the most part this seemed unlikely. He would then generalize the construction and learn to substitute other appropriate forms in the same construction. [1973, 89]

Krashen and Scarcella review some of the recent literature on the appearance of formulaic speech in language learning and claim to show that formulaic speech is, in fact, a dead end as far as the evolution of creative language is concerned. Although they acknowledge Wong Fillmore's evidence for formulaic breakdown, they raise the question whether language is generally acquired under circumstances similar to those in her study: "Clearly, the sort of early output demands [Wong] Fillmore's subjects had imposed on them, and the routinized [i.e., formulaic] predictable input are not present in most language acquisition situations" (1978, 295). They do, however, agree that both the nature of the input speech and the kind of speech expected from the child may affect the strategies a learner employs:

As we have seen in first language and second language acquisition by children, the "gestalt" route is used by acquirers under similar conditions: where input is complex, and where conversational demands are present, acquirers may tend to use whole utterances in conversationally appropriate places without a full grasp of their internal structure. [295]

They deny, however, that formulaic speech learned under such circumstances leads to the acquisition of creative language. Wong Fillmore, on the other hand, draws the opposite conclusion, asserting that in fact

the analyses the learners perform are on those things which are most available to them – the well-practiced and familiar expressions they find in their own speech repertoires. How much more reasonable this seems than to assume that the language learner can somehow apprehend the fast-fading message produced by someone else, figure out what it means and how it is put together, and then relate it to similar utterances he has heard. Instead, what the children have to work with are expressions which make sense to them already, at least in the context of use. They know how an utterance can be used, even if they do not always know how it segments, what all of its individual components are, or how they function. Eventually they manage to sort out the parts of these utterances and to discover what other items might substitute for them.

[1976, 301]

Krashen and Scarcella's doubts about the relevance of formulaic speech for language acquisition seem to stem from a pedagogical point of view rather than from the evidence they consider, since they grudgingly acknowledge the force of Wong Fillmore's study. They are, however, primarily concerned with the teaching of second languages in the classroom, and they raise valid objections to the audio-lingual method (a "pure formulaic" approach) as the sole method to be used, since it provides so little input for the creative construction process (297–8). Perhaps a crude formulaic approach has been overused in the second-language classroom, whereas possible refinements have not been sufficiently explored (see 5.3 for further discussion). In first-language acquisition research, however, this strategy has not really been recognized as a possible factor in the process. Wong Fillmore's work presents a challenge to reexamine first-language learning to determine the true role of formulaic speech in this situation (1976, 302). Much of the rest of this book will be concerned with how the formulaic approach can be integrated with the traditional assumption of increasing size in language development.

Krashen and Scarcella claim that since routines (i.e., speech formulas) appear to be immune to rules when they are first acquired (consider, e.g., the example just quoted from Brown and Hanlon of *what's that?* which did not get changed to *what that is?*), "this clearly implies that routines are part of a system that is separate from the process generating rule-governed, propositional language" (1978, 286). If this claim merely means that routines are not generated but are reproduced as wholes, then it is not saying very much – it is just a consequence of the definition of "routine."

If on the other hand the emphasis is on the separateness of the collection of routines from the system of generative processes, then these two are no more separate than the lexicon is from the generative process. For there is no evidence that what the linguist recognizes as unanalyzed routines are recognized and stored by the child any differently from items that we would call single words. Hence routines are only "separate" from the generative system insofar as the lexicon is separate. Reproducing a routine is in no way different from reproducing any other single item from the lexicon.

To focus on this separateness, moreover, is to miss the more interesting point, namely, on the one hand the relation between rules as they are induced and on the other hand the items, particularly the routines, stored in the lexicon. I will suggest that items in the lexicon are subject to analysis by the rules as they are induced and those items that yield to such analysis may lose their status as unitary items of storage. This in fact must be the main process used by children initially breaking into the language system. The "little units" and "big units" that Krashen and Scarcella claim are handled by separate systems will be seen to be two sides of the same coin.

2 The initial extraction problem and the one-unit stage

In the previous chapter I introduced the notion that the learning of "units," which may not necessarily correspond to the ultimate constituents of the adult's language, is the first step in a child's acquisition of the language, even though the recognition by the linguist of these units in the child's speech may present some methodological, but not insuperable, difficulties. What I wish to examine next are the circumstances surrounding the acquisition of these units. In particular, how do children get hold of these earliest units? Obviously they must extract them from the streams of speech that they hear around them. The problem of doing this is what I call "the initial extraction problem." In this chapter my focus will first be on what strategies children may use to attack this problem. Then I will look at what factors may produce the observed variation in individual children's solutions, that is, in the size and types of units they extract.

2.1. Extraction of early units and the "utterance is a word" strategy

If language learners need to extract linguistic units from heard speech, what sort of knowledge and processing strategies must they bring to this task? In particular, do children have to know how to recognize what a "word" is in order to know how much to extract? Or might they at first not be constrained to respect adult word boundaries? In the light of the evidence already presented that early units may vary in size from words to whole phrases, I propose that children approach this task with the simplest strategy that can get the process started: They consider any utterance a potential lexical entry and copy and store it whole. The question what the child is to consider an "utterance" in an unknown language will be refined later in this section. It may not, as we shall see, always coincide with the adult's concept of an utterance.

Although the proposal that children may use whole utterances as their

16

initial lexical entries has the advantage of allowing us simultaneously to account for both *one-word* and *formulaic* speech, the objection can be raised that many utterances are too long for small children to handle. Before proceeding with a discussion of other extraction strategies, let us first deal with this memory problem.

What would such an objection be really based on, besides our general awareness that early language productions tend to be severely limited in length? Is there evidence that young children's memories are not yet developed to the point where they can remember very many items (or very much of anything), whether nonlinguistic or linguistic? Or is there evidence that children's memories are limited specifically with respect to linguistic material?

There is some evidence that, as far as nonlinguistic material is concerned, younger children's memories are no more limited than those of older children. Thus Olson (1973, 150–1) reviews several experiments that involve children's recall of nonverbal materials (e.g., their memory for magazine pictures); when the children were tested in such a way that nonverbal cues could be employed in giving responses, younger children (around age 3) remembered as much as older children (of various ages). He concludes that younger children's apparent memory limitations are due to an inability to encode the responses verbally rather than to an inability to remember numbers of items.

Snow (1981b) also reviews evidence that young children are perfectly capable of remembering complex events for long intervals. For instance, DeLoache and Brown (1979) found that 18-month-olds could remember the locations of toys for several hours. Even more compelling is Snow's diary evidence: Her 2-year-old son was observed to remember very specific (but mostly trivial) incidents over periods of time ranging from three days to two months.

If children's memories for nonlinguistic material are not limited, what about linguistic material? It has in fact been observed that even young children can be very good at remembering and reproducing fairly long chunks of speech. Thus, Bloom notes,

the children's ability to remember complex linguistic material was often impressive – as evidenced by the production of stereotype model sentences that had no analogue in the child's grammar; for example, "who has that book?, Kathryn has that book" at Kathryn I [1;9]. An even more striking example was Eric's ability to "recite" accurately from memory long passages of text in his favorite story books, turning the pages at the appropriate juncture, when he was two and one-half years old. But he was unable to answer specific questions about the text, and certain phrase structures he recited – sentence adverbials for example – did not appear in his spontaneous utterances. [1970, 168–9]

The evidence therefore shows that some children can in fact remember whole utterances, some of which can be quite long. It does not seem unreasonable, then, to attribute to all children the strategy of extracting at least selected whole utterances.

In order to make more concrete the proposed extraction process, I will present it as a series of heuristics for processing linguistic input. These heuristics are modeled after Slobin's Operating Principles (1973) for acquisition of syntax, but they apply to a much earlier stage of language acquisition. The two most basic heuristics are

EXTRACT1.   Extract whole utterances from the speech stream surrounding you and remember them together with salient features of the situational context.

EXTRACT2.   Store the whole unit as a single entry in your lexicon.

Determining what is an "utterance" is influenced by saliency properties of the input speech and by early limitations on the amount of information the child is able to pay attention to at once. These constraints make it necessary for the child to enlist further heuristics to focus attention on selected aspects of input speech, in particular to delimit stretches of speech and to select which of these are to be remembered.

One heuristic that limits the choice of utterances is based on saliency of meaning:

EX:MEANING.   Extract and remember sound sequences that have a clear connection to a clear context.

The problem of delimiting utterances (i.e., chunks to be extracted) is dealt with by a set of heuristics that make use of salient properties of the input speech. Probably the most salient property is the distinction between silence and speech. The first delimiting heuristic I propose is

EX:SILENCE.   An utterance is bounded by silence.

Children have been observed to extract, presumably on the basis of this heuristic, single words (when they are bounded by silence), whole phrases (bounded by silence), and even two run-on phrases (bounded by silence but not sufficiently separated by silence). These three cases are respectively illustrated by the following three examples from the literature.

1.   Nelson (1973, 104):

Mother: Jane. Here's a bottle. Where's the bottle? Here's a bottle.
Jane: Wah-wah.
Mother: Bottle.
Jane: Bah-bah.

2.   Peters (field notes):

Minh's mother frequently exclaimed "Look at that!" to him and [dùkədǽt] was one of Minh's first utterances that I could associate with any certainty with a known target.

3.   Clark (1977, 350):

Adam: Squeeze.
Adult: Squeeze? You squeeze.
Adam: Squeeze you squeeze.

Another salient phonological property is intonation contour. It is used by the following heuristic:

EX:SUPRASEG.   An utterance is a suprasegmentally delimited stretch of speech.

In her study of the prosodic characteristics of American mothers' speech to 2-year-olds, Garnica found that more sentence-final pitch contours were rising than in these same mothers' speech to 5-year-olds or adults. She hypothesizes that these rising pitch terminals "may be used to cue the child to the location of sentence boundaries" (1977, 84). Such information, then, would feed strategy EX:SUPRASEG.

Other aspects of intonation may also provide useful clues for children. In particular, the characteristic intonation of question tags may also support this heuristic. Adam Clark at 2;3.8 extracted *isn't it*:

Adult: That's an elephant, isn't it?
         What is it?
         (A minute or two later)
Adam: Intit.   (Adam continued to call elephants "intits" for several weeks and was impervious to corrections.)   [Clark 1977, 349]

MacWhinney labels this early strategy "intonational packaging" and suggests that "early forms will take the shape of units which are separately packaged by intonation in the input" (1978, 10). In languages other than English, stress and tone patterns that recur predictably may serve as segmentation clues. Thus, in Hungarian, where main stress always occurs on the first syllable of a word, children rarely make word-segmentation errors (MacWhinney 1976, 389).

Another salient phonological property is the intonation contour itself:

EX:TUNE.   An utterance is a speech tune or melody.

Note that this heuristic results in the extraction of the intonation contour itself as an utterance, rather than in the extraction of a segmental stream delimited by that contour, as with the previous heuristic. EX:TUNE is the same as the strategy I have elsewhere called "learning the tune before the words" (Peters 1974), where the "tune" (i.e., the intonational contour) of a particular phrase seems to have been more salient, and hence more memorable, than its segmental phonemes. English phrases that can have such characteristic tunes include *uh-oh! look at that! what's that?* In order to produce carriers for these tunes Minh often mumbled, using nonsense syllables or poor approximations of the adult sequence of segmental phonemes (Peters 1977).

The final phonological property that seems relevant here is rhythmic pattern as manifested in stress, vowel length, and/or number of syllables:

EX:RHYTHM.   An utterance is a rhythmic pattern of speech.

There is ample evidence from early language production for the importance of such a rhythm-based heuristic. It is manifested in the appearance of "filler syllables," which seem to be incompletely analyzed syllables that are nevertheless reproduced in a "fuzzy" form that maintains the meter of a particular phrase. Such syllables have been reported in the early productions of children learning English (Bloom 1970; Braine 1976; Peters 1977), Spanish and Cakchiquel (Tolbert 1978), Turkish (Ekmeci 1979; Slobin & Aksu 1980), and SiSwati (Kunene 1979).

It should be noted that in any of these examples more than one heuristic could have had a role, although the heuristic it is placed with is probably the most relevant. It is well to remember that these saliency-based heuristics interact with and mutually reinforce each other. Thus an utterance that is at once frequent, often bounded by silence, and possessed of characteristic rhythm and intonation contours is likely to be much more memorable (and thus earlier learned) than an utterance distinguished by only one of these characteristics.

2.2.   Factors affecting the size of extracted units

In reviewing the literature on early language acquisition one finds that some but not all of children's early language productions (their first "words") are targeted on single adult words. Moreover, this variation can be found both within and across children. A number of terms have been coined to describe the opposing extremes of such variation, extremes that are usually described in terms of constellations of typical observed characteristics. Nelson (1973) has used the terms "Referential" and "Expressive," Peters (1977) has used "Analytic" and "Gestalt," and Horgan (1980) has used "Noun-lovers" and "Noun-leavers." These extremes are generally considered to define the end points of continua along which most children are ranged, very few being clearly at one pole or the other.

What factors in the child's language-learning situation may be responsible for the observed variations in the size of children's first productions – and by inference in the size of the units they first extract? At least four such factors can be cited: (1) the child's communicative needs, that is, the functions language must serve for her or him, (2) the type of speech the child is exposed to, (3) the type of speech that is expected from the child by her or his caretakers, and (4) the child's individual neurological endowment, which may also underlie any idiosyncrasies of personality.

As we look at each of these factors in turn we must keep in mind that, although each can be described independently, they all operate simultaneously and interact in complex ways. Not only may the picture be somewhat different between any two children, but even within a particular child these factors may combine in different ways in different situations to produce observable variations. Furthermore, this very complexity makes it difficult to disentangle the factors for separate inspection: There is no clear priority and hence no easy place to begin. Bearing this in mind, let us plunge in.

2.2.1. The functions of language for the child

Although the field of linguistics proper focuses on the forms of speech, socio- and ethnolinguistics have been concerned with its uses as well, recognizing that conveying information is only one of many potential functions. Halliday (1973), in particular, has identified a whole range of language functions, including Interpersonal, Regulatory, and Interactional, all of which involve various kinds of social relations. In fact, almost any utterance is directed at achieving more than one communicative goal: "I'm cold" may convey the information that I am indeed cold, while simultaneously requesting that something be done about it (e.g., shutting the window) and indicating that for some social reason I am unwilling to ask my hearer directly to do it.

In spite of such inherent complexity for adults, when children start to learn how the language system works, they may begin by focusing more on one function than on another. Nelson (1973) has proposed that some children decide that their primary need for language is for talking about things (the Referential function of language), whereas other children decide that language is primarily useful for social interaction (the Expressive function). Since Referential children tend to learn names for things and people, their early vocabularies contain many nouns, whereas Expressive children are likelier to learn the verbs, adjectives, and especially the social phrases (such as *hi*, *thank you*, *oh boy*, *all gone*) useful for interacting with others. Note that these are tendencies, not all-or-none phenomena. Thus Nelson found that before the eighteen children she studied reached the fifty-word vocabulary level, "the number of phrases produced by the R[eferential] group during this period ranged from 0 to 5 (mean 2.4) while those of the E[xpressive] group ranged from 6 to 18 (12.6)" (1973, 22).

Halliday, too, has proposed a functional split in early language use between

Mathetic and Pragmatic (1975, 17–28). Mathetic language contributes to a child's learning about the environment, whereas Pragmatic language includes the instrumental, regulatory, and expressive-conative uses that contribute to interpersonal relations. This dichotomy seems to correspond rather well to Nelson's Referential versus Expressive.

Furthermore, two strategies of early language production that I have labeled Analytic and Gestalt (Peters 1977) seem to be fostered differentially by the need to use language mathetically (referentially) and the need to use it pragmatically (expressively). An Analytic utterance is "the nice neat one-word utterance" that over time "slowly [increases] . . . in closeness to the adult target" (563); in Gestalt utterances the segmental fidelity is poor, although "the combination of number of syllables, stress, intonation, and such segments as [can] be distinguished [combine] to give a very good impression of sentencehood" (564). My observation was that for Minh, the child in that study, Analytic speech was generally used in referential contexts, such as naming pictures in a book, whereas Gestalt speech tended to be used in more sociable contexts, such as playing with his brother, or in commenting about objects rather than naming them (566). Note that Mathetic/Referential seems to have to do with cognitive development and learning about the structure of the world outside the self. Older children, however, such as those in Wong Fillmore's study of 5- to 7-year-olds acquiring English as their second language (1976), are well beyond this stage of cognitive development: They do not need to learn about the world, but they do need social interaction; hence they tend first to acquire Interpersonal/Expressive language.

As Nelson's data suggest, the purpose for which children use their language can affect the kind and size of initial units that they tend to extract from the speech stream. The cognitive (Mathetic) need to label aspects of their daily world (a need that may be fostered by the kind of input speech and expectations about language use that they encounter; see 2.2.2) can motivate them to try to extract such labels from the speech stream. In fact, children soon learn some means of eliciting labels from adults; it may be a point and a grunt, or it may be a formula such as Minh's [əsæ] or [sæ] ('what's that?'). Children are also often heard to label objects aloud to themselves with no attempt to communicate to others, as if the association of the sound with the object were part of a cognitive process of recognition. Since most labels tend to be single words or tightly tied phrases (e.g., *choochoo train*, *rocking horse*, kittycat), the result is that Referential or Mathetic-oriented children seem to produce (and presumably extract) more short, Analytic utterances.

On the other hand, the children's need to interact with their environment, both to get others to do things they are unable to do alone (regulatory) and to acknowledge the presence of an important caretaker (interpersonal), will drive them to extract from the speech stream the necessary language for conducting such pragmatic interactions. Since this type of interaction tends to be conducted, at least in English, through multi-word formulas or sentences (e.g., *give me that*, *you do it*, *nice to see you*, *I want*, *that's mine*), the result is that Expressive or Pragmatic-oriented children seem to produce (and presumably extract) proportionally more long, Gestalt utterances.

Although it may be possible to classify most children at the early stages of language learning into dichotomous categories such as those just discussed, such classifications will necessarily be rough and based on some sort of predominant strategy the child seems to be using. But Nelson reminds us that since "most children learning language learn to use it in a variety of contexts for a variety of purposes, most children will exhibit aspects of both formulaic and analytic approaches in their early language . . . It appears that children can master languages in either way and probably in both at once" (1981, 182–3).

2.2.2. *Input speech*

Since the speech heard by children constitutes the primary data they have available from which to discover the workings of the language to which they are exposed, it is reasonable to ask whether variations in input speech might be reflected in observable variations in the type of speech first produced by different children, and by inference in the size of units they first extract. Although numerous studies on language input have appeared in the last ten years, the kind of evidence that is relevant to variation is barely beginning to appear. There are two types of reasons for this: theoretical and methodological.

The theoretical reasons have to do with the focus of most input studies, which have generally been concerned either with interaction between mother and child (e.g., how babies younger than 1 year learn to take conversational turns; see Sachs 1977a; Snow 1977) or with linguistic support for emerging syntax in children 18 months or older (Cross 1977; Garnica 1977; Shatz & Gelman 1977), rather than with extraction of early units (but see Nelson 1973). Even those studies which include children in the crucial (for extraction) 10- to 20-month-old range have been more interested in the effects of input on syntactic measures such as number of noun or verb phrases per utterance than on size and type of units extracted (e.g., Newport, Gleitman, & Gleitman 1977).

One likely cause for the lack of interest in extraction variables is that little variation was noticed, probably owing to methodological factors. Thus the observed mother–child dyads have been predominantly from the middle or upper-middle class in English-speaking communities (United States: Garnica

1977; Newport et al. 1977; Phillips 1973; England: Snow 1977; Australia: Cross 1977); the children have tended to be first-born (Snow; Phillips); and the recording situation has often been either a soundproof laboratory play-room (Garnica; Newport et al.; Phillips) or the child's playroom at home (Cross). There is growing evidence, however, that this homogeneity of cul-ture, social class, birth order, and recording situation may have conspired to produce homogeneity in the kinds of language used by both mothers and children – a homogeneity that is not generalizable to caretaker–child interac-tions in other cultures, social classes, or interactive settings.

Nelson was the first researcher to notice these methodological limitations. The group of children she studied consisted of eighteen middle-class Ameri-can children of whom eleven were first-born and seven were second-born (1973, 60). The parents' educational levels ranged from high school to pro-fessional degrees. The children were between 10 and 15 months old at the beginning of her project, and almost all data collection was done in the children's homes. One of her interests was early vocabulary development, and much of the data were collected in diary form by the children's mothers during their normal daily activities. Nelson noted a tendency for first-borns to be Referential (seven to four) and for second-borns to be Expressive (four to three), although this was not statistically significant (60). But when she also took the parents' educational level into account she found that *"all of the firstborn children of the most highly educated families (those with college educa-tions and better) were found in the R[eferential] group"* (61, emphasis hers). She goes on to comment:

As this is the pool from which the vast majority of previous samples employed in the study of early language development has derived, it is an important cautionary finding. It indicates that characteristics thought to be general – even universal – may be con-fined to a group that differs importantly and systematically from other groups within the general population. [61]

Nelson, then, gave us the first hints that there might be both cultural and familial factors that affect input speech, which in turn might affect a child's route to language.

More recently, three ethnographically based language-acquisition studies, carried out in very different cultural settings, have shown that input speech can indeed be very different from that observed among middle-class English-speaking mothers. These studies are Schieffelin's (1979) study done among the Kaluli of New Guinea, Ochs's (1980) study done in American Samoa, and Heath's (1982, 1983) study of a black community in the Piedmont Carolinas.

Schieffelin found that the Kaluli are very conscious of the language devel-opment of their children and deliberately try to teach them to speak by direct instruction, that is, by telling them appropriate things to say in specific circumstances. Such speech, however, is normal adult speech; in fact, the Kaluli find the idea of "baby talk" dismaying. Even young babies are seen as "individuals with intentions, ideas, and identities" (1979, 108), and it is felt to be important for mothers to help these identities emerge, at first by speaking for their infants, then by instructing their toddlers in how to interact in appropriate social and linguistic ways. Although some Kaluli instruction takes place in dyadic situations (when only mother and child are interacting), a much larger portion takes place in triadic situations, in which the mother coaches the child on what to say to a third party. What are the effects of such language on the size of early language units? Since Schieffelin deliberately chose children who were beginning to put words together, they were all beyond the initial extraction stage. Thus she gives no data on their successes or failures in segmenting adult-sized words out of such speech. One can speculate, however, that this unsimplified type of input might foster extraction strategies different from those encouraged by mainstream American input.

One thing that struck Ochs about caretaker speech in American Samoa was the absence of the expansions of children's utterances so typical of American mothers' speech. After comparing Samoan and American middle-class beliefs about status, rights to speak, and capability to act intentionally, she concludes that Samoan caretakers do not expand their charges' utterances because young children are not considered really capable of communicating intentionally. It is also not appropriate for a (higher-status) caregiver to try to accommodate a (lower-status) child's perspective by offering confirmation checks (in the form of expansions) about what the child might have intended to say. On the contrary, much of caretaker speech consists of providing social instruction for the young child, including elicitation of imitations of people's names and socially appropriate greetings, questions, and so on (1980, 32). In this way Samoan caretaker speech seems similar to that among the Kaluli, although the Kaluli have a strong language-instruction component in their caretaker talk that seems to be absent among the Samoans (37). Samoan input is also similar to Kaluli input in that it is not marked by "baby talk lexicon, special morphological modifications (diminutives, etc.), simpler syntactic constructions or constructions of reduced length" (36). On the other hand, since much of the caretaking in Samoa is done not by the children's mother but by the older girls of the family, there may be other, as yet unexplored variables in the type of speech heard by Samoan children. These features might make their extraction problem somewhat different from that faced by the American child.

Heath's study (1982, 1983) includes observation of language learning in a small all-black residential community in the Piedmont Carolinas. In this community, which she calls Trackton, adults do not think of children as conversational partners until they are skilled enough to be "seen as realistic sources of information and competent partners in talk" (1982, 114). Since Trackton mothers, like the Kaluli and Samoan mothers, usually have other, more skilled, conversational partners available, they are not limited to talking with toddlers. But neither do they exclude young children from adult talk. Direct communication with infants is primarily nonverbal, since they are carried about all day. Linguistically the children are exposed to streams of talk that continually flow past them. And their first attempts at speaking (between 12 and 24 months) tend to consist of imitations of the ends of overheard phrases or sentences. Heath's examples of such imitations show children picking up in this way chunks that are several morphemes long. It seems, not surprisingly, that given such input they extract, not single words, but longer chunks that are probably intonationally salient as well as intonationally delimited.

In addition to the overall cultural patterns, factors within the family may result in differences in the type of speech heard by the child, leading to variation in initial extraction behavior. For instance, the influence of sibling speech may be very important for second and later children, especially in cultures in which the nuclear family is the rule. This is an area that has hardly been touched; the only study I have seen is Montgomery (1977), which, since it is the study of only one sibling pair, raises more questions than it answers. The questions, however, are intriguing, and more systematic investigation of this area is needed. Montgomery finds that

parental estimations of the advanced level of acquisition of the second child [relative to their estimation of that of their first child at the same age] are not verified in the data. In the analysis of imitation data it is found that the child who imitates . . . the sibling is indeed making a great number of significant and situationally appropriate remarks, thereby giving the illusory impression of advanced competence. [4]

The presence of an older child in the family provides the younger learner with a model of how to interact with others, a model that may well be absent for firstborns. Thus, by 14 months, Minh had learned the "summons-response routine," which was frequently modeled for him by his older brother: He frequently tried this out by calling out "Mommy!" and his mother dutifully and predictably responded with either "What?" or "Huh?" Minh's linguistic development was still so rudimentary that he could not make effective use of this routine to introduce a topic of talk, but he clearly knew that its function was to get his mother's attention.

Older siblings may also provide models for pronoun usage, modeling phrases with incorporated pronouns that younger learners first extract as chunks (e.g., *That's mine!*, *I dunno*, *I don't wanna*). Clark notes: "The area of pronouns would seem to be one in which first children are at a particular disadvantage. Since they do not have other children playing the same role as themselves with respect to their parents, they do not have the same opportunity for modeling utterances" (1977, 352). And Nelson observes:

The mother who has a 3- or 4-year-old to cope with, as well as a 1- or 2-year-old, will use characteristically different language in interaction with both children than will the mother who has only one child of 1 or 2 years. A larger percentage of the function of language that the younger sibling hears is likely to be directive and centered around the child's own activities – to be, in effect, pragmatic and expressive. Thus the child is likely to conclude that language is a pragmatic medium that is useful for social control and social exchange, and this conclusion is likely to be shored up by exchanges with siblings. [1981, 181]

Since English does not inflect either nouns or verbs for gender, we have not noticed how the sex of a child can affect the (adult) composition of early extracted units. Hebrew, however, does inflect verbs for gender. Berman (1978) found that her daughter Shelli's first verbs were extracted from the feminine forms that she heard addressed to herself, for .example, *kli* ($<$ *tistakli*) 'look! (fem.)', or *shvi* 'sit down (fem.)'. Shelli used these forms when addressing or referring to members of either sex.

Another source of variation in initial extraction behavior has so far escaped notice because the range of interactions during which data have been collected has been so limited. As already noted, the recordings on which many of the input studies were based were made in playroom settings, often in laboratory playrooms on university campuses. During these interactions the mothers were generally encouraged to focus on the speech and/or behavior of their children; often they were not told until after the recordings had been made that the purpose of the study was to look at their own speech (e.g., Garnica 1977; Newport et al. 1977). Such recording conditions conspire to orient middle-class American mothers to try to elicit speech and certain kinds of direction-following behavior from their children. In these dyadic interactions there is much labeling of objects and attributes, along with repetitions and rephrasings of directions. This kind of Mathetic/Referential speech on the parts of the mothers is, on the whole, optimally structured to foster extractions of small units, usually one word long, that are Referential in nature.

But is this a representative sample of the kind of linguistic input that these middle-class American children receive? In the course of their daily lives do they not also participate in other, more social, types of interactions, especially at mealtimes, bedtime, diaper changing, or the arrival and departure of visitors? Although triadic interactions such as those found among the Kaluli may occur much more rarely in the mainstream English-speaking population, partly because of the relatively small family sizes, there is some evidence that some of these do occur, at least in the context of teaching social skills (Gleason & Weintraub 1978). Systematic efforts to collect such speech have not yet been carried out, though studies of specific routines, such as the trick-or-treat routine at Halloween (Gleason & Weintraub 1976), have been done.

This omission, though partly owing to lack of awareness regarding the potential importance of such routines to the language-acquisition process, is also due to difficulties in collecting these kinds of data. It is much easier and less invasive of the subjects' privacy to bring a mother and child into an acoustically treated laboratory playroom for an hour of recorded interaction than it is to try to record the language used in the regular daily life of the home. Collection of the latter kinds of data requires, at a minimum, that the researcher come to the home and record for periods of several hours in a single day (see, e.g., Bloom 1970; Miller 1979; Ochs 1980; Schieffelin 1979) in order to capture a variety of interactions between caretaker and child, including the comings and goings of any visitors. Even better would be well-designed diary studies supplemented by selective audio recording in which the parent acted as principal data collector.[4] Although it may be more difficult to enforce objectivity in data collection by parents, these may be the only kinds of data that will give a true picture of the range of input that children really receive. And if social routines, which involve Pragmatic/ Expressive speech, foster the extraction of longer units, we are missing half of the picture until we carry out such studies.

2.2.3. *Expectations regarding children's speech participation and productions*

The child's linguistic environment consists not only of the input speech, but also of a culturally determined set of expectations regarding appropriate language use and acceptable language style. These expectations have not been much discussed until very recently because investigators have tended to conduct language-acquisition research within their own cultures (for obvious reasons having to do with comprehensibility and access), and hence have not been aware of the ways in which differences in such expectations could affect the process of language development. In particular, these expectations form the unconscious basis of feedback from caretakers to children concerning whether their early vocalizations "count" as language. Such feedback may influence not only the size and types of units extracted but also children's perceptions of appropriate occasions of use. With the rise in interest in

---

[4] Braunwald & Brislin (1979) give excellent guidelines for designing such studies, and Ferrier (1978) is a nice example of a diary-based study that is able to link child and adult utterances with social and physical contexts.

ethnographies of speaking, linguists have become more aware of the cultural expectations surrounding adult language use (see, e.g., the studies in Bauman & Sherzer 1974 and in Gumperz & Hymes 1972), but it was not until recently that such ethnographic concerns were specifically taken up by those interested in children's early language (Blount 1972; Heath forthcoming; Miller 1979; Ochs 1980; Schieffelin 1979). Although there is not yet a great deal of information on how such expectations differ from culture to culture (but see Schieffelin & Eisenberg 1981), it is worth looking in some detail at what currently exists, because of the potential power of such expectations to influence the size of early extractions. We will begin closest to home.

There is growing evidence that there is a single widespread set of expectations regarding early language use that is characteristic of, but not limited to, middle-class American mothers. These expectations, largely summarized from Heath's description of middle-class parents in the Piedmont Carolinas (forthcoming, chap. 6) include the following:

1. That babies are potential conversational partners as soon as they are born (and perhaps even in the womb), although their conversational turns may have to be supplied for them;

2. That systematic modifications of the language addressed to babies, modifications producing what is known as "baby talk" (see Ferguson 1977 for details), facilitate communication with them;

3. That babies' early vocalizations are interpretable as intentional conversational turns with a meaning deducible from the context;

4. That such vocalizations warrant repetition and expansion by the caretaker, who is usually the mother;

5. That it is important, through modeling and contextualization, to teach babies the proper labels for the people and things in their environment;

6. That the production of such labels can and should be encouraged through contextualized interactive question-and-answer routines, such as "What's that? That's an X. That's right. X" (see Ninio & Bruner 1978 for details);

7. That babies' first words are likely to be names, either of people (especially Daddy) or of objects.

To me it seems clear that this set of unconscious assumptions is optimally designed to foster the extraction of units that are exactly one word in length and that have a Mathetic/Referential function. This fostering is primarily effected through the dual mechanisms of provision of labels (6) and expectation of the production of labels (7). Once we have laid these assumptions out for inspection we can see that they underlie much (although not all) of the caretaker talk in middle-class English-speaking families. Berman has observed similar labeling routines in Israeli middle-class families.[5]

[5] Personal communication.

Of course, even within a particular culture there are individual variations among mothers in what they expect about their children's early language. Nelson observed that the mothers she studied could be categorized as Accepting or Rejecting on the basis of whether they accepted or rejected the linguistic productions of their children as legitimate speech (1973, 103–4). Some mothers tended to accept as language practically everything their children produced, whereas others tended not to hear their children's vocalizations as real speech. These are the extreme cases; other mothers presumably fell in between, although Nelson felt that she could classify all eighteen of the mothers she studied as Accepting or Rejecting.

Lieven, too, found that two middle-class English mothers whom she observed differed quite noticeably in their manners of interacting linguistically with their toddlers. Kate, a firstborn child, was 18 months old at the start of the study, and Beth, a secondborn, was 20 months old. According to Lieven, "The speech of both mothers to their children showed many of the features which have by now become familiar" (1978, 178). And yet Kate's mother was observed to make more efforts to communicate with her daughter than Beth's mother: She responded to Kate's comprehensible utterances 81 percent of the time (as opposed to 46 percent for Beth's mother); she was more likely to interrupt an ongoing conversation with an adult in order to make such responses; and her responses tended to be geared to extending the communicative interaction rather than simply acknowledging her daughter's utterance. The relevant underlying assumptions here involve the child's role as a legitimate conversational partner and the acceptability of the child's utterances as real speech. It is noteworthy that the children's language was observed to differ markedly: Kate was much like Nelson's Referential children, whereas Beth was more Expressive. And they "appeared to be using language for different ends. Kate talked slowly and coherently about things happening around her and objects in her environment while Beth devoted more time using her speech to try and engage her mother's interest" (178). Thus it seems likely that these mothers' differing expectations about their daughters' language influenced the children's strategies for breaking into the language system.

If we look at studies of language learning in working-class American families we find that, at least in some groups, the underlying assumptions are roughly the same as those just outlined. This is the case for the community of white mill workers in South Carolina described by Heath (1983, chap. 4). Although Miller's (1979) study of three white working-class families in South Baltimore did not start when the children were young enough to be producing their first words, one can find evidence there for assumptions 4, 5, and 6.

On the other hand, Heath's ethnographic study of black mill workers in South Carolina (1983, chap. 3) reveals a radically different set of assumptions, which can be summarized as follows:

1. That children are not potential conversational partners until they have achieved enough skill to get the floor and introduce an intelligible topic into a conversation;

2. That language rarely needs to be addressed *to* babies, although there may be much talk *about* babies in their presence;

3. That babies' early vocalizations are interpretable as noise rather than as language: Smiles and coos are to be rewarded with nuzzles and physical play;

4. Vocalizations that middle-class mothers would interpret as "words" are not worthy of a response designed to further communication because young children have no need to try to communicate their wishes or needs to their knowing caretakers;

5. That there are no unique labels for either people or objects: People may have multiple names or nicknames, each negotiated with particular (sets of) individuals, and similarly, what one calls an object may depend on the context;

6. That children cannot be taught to talk by adults, but rather must "come up" on their own: When they have something to say they will say it;

7. That children, especially boys, will first start to interact linguistically in socially defined situations, often involving challenges to their status as individuals or possessors of goods.

These assumptions are clearly very different from the middle-class set. And if we look at yet other cultures we find an even greater range of expectations. In our discussion of variations in the kinds of input speech that children hear we have already looked briefly at beliefs in two cultures, Kaluli and Samoan, which differ markedly from our own. If we try to extract a set of expectations regarding children's rights to participate in conversations and the nature of their early speech productions from the reports on these cultures (Ochs 1980; Schieffelin 1979), we find numerous differences from either of the sets just presented. Let us look briefly at the range of variation that is found when we broaden our scope in this way.[6]

1. Rights of the child to participate in conversations:
   a. Children are born with such rights: middle-class English-speaking

---

[6] Schieffelin & Eisenberg (1981) review the data on these cultures as well as on several others, for which the data are more meager. I have decided to include here only the Kaluli and Samoan data, and in a few instances inferences from Blount's study of the Luo in Africa (1972), since I have the most details on these cultures and since these additions broaden the picture sufficiently without losing us in a morass of detail. The interested reader is urged to consult Schieffelin & Eisenberg and the references therein. It should further be borne in mind that since both the Samoan and Kaluli studies focused on the emergence of syntax, neither has much information on the extraction of early units or on the cultural beliefs surrounding these early extractions.

  b. Children must achieve such rights through the acquisition of
      sociolinguistic competence: Trackton
  c. Children must achieve such rights through the acquisition of age and
      status (i.e., children should be seen and not heard): Samoa, Luo
2.   Modification of talk to babies:
  a. Talk to babies must be modified in order to promote comprehension:
      middle-class English-speaking
  b. Talk to babies should not be modified; correct speech should be
      modeled: Kaluli
  c. Caretakers don't talk to babies: Trackton
3.   Meaning of babies' early vocalizations:
  a. They are interpretable: middle-class English-speaking
  b. They are of no consequence: Trackton, Samoa
4.   Response to babies' vocalizations:
  a. They should be repeated and expanded when possible: middle-class
      English-speaking
  b. They should be accepted but not modified: Kaluli?
  c. They should be ignored: Trackton, Samoa?
5.   Language skills that need to be explicitly taught:
  a. Labels for people and things: middle-class English-speaking, Luo,
      Kaluli (to a lesser extent)
  b. Appropriate ways to interact socially: Kaluli, middle-class English-
      speaking (a limited set of routines only), Samoa (calling-out routines)
  c. People's names: Samoa
  d. None: Trackton
6.   Language-teaching mechanisms:
  a. Question-and-answer routines: middle-class English-speaking
  b. Direct instruction to "say X": Kaluli, middle-class English-speaking (to
      a lesser extent: social routines and names), Samoa (calling-out
      routines)
  c. Children will talk when they have something to say: Trackton
7.   Babies' first "real" language:
  a. Names of people or things: middle-class English-speaking
  b. Specific words: Kaluli.[7]

What is the effect of these differences in expectations on children's early
extraction strategies? At the moment it is still hard to tell, since the relevant
data are lacking. We have one hint, however, in Heath's observation that
Trackton children's early productions are imitations of chunks lifted from the
ends of sentences overheard in surrounding adult conversations. It would
seem that a Trackton type of environment might foster an Expressive or
Gestalt type of early strategy. The ways that adult expectations about children's early language behavior can influence the type and size of the earliest
extractions clearly need investigation.

---

[7] Kaluli children are not considered to have begun talking until they are heard to use two specific
words: *nɔ* 'mother' and *bo* 'breast', regardless of whether they can already use other words
(Schieffelin & Eisenberg 1981, 14).

2.2.4. Individual personality and neurology

The fourth and least tangible factor that may affect early extraction strategies pertains to individual personality and neurological differences. Such differences may explain, for instance, why some of Nelson's subjects turned out to be predominantly Referential in spite of having mothers who both produced and expected Expressive speech, and vice versa. And how else can we explain why the firstborn daughter of an academic American couple clearly preferred an Expressive/Gestalt/Noun-leaver strategy (which persisted at least until age 5), whereas their secondborn son was a Noun-lover (Horgan 1980)? There also seem to be otherwise unexplainable individual differences among young children in their propensity to imitate speech heard around them. For some children imitations occur in as few as 2 percent of the utterances they produce, whereas for others imitations occur in up to 40 percent of their utterances (Snow 1981b, 10–11, tab. 3). Such an individual motivation to imitate could have a noticeable effect on the sizes and types of early extractions.

Individual differences may also be relevant in accounting for some of the individual variation in the learning styles of adult second-language learners. Thus Krashen observes that "some people seem not to utilize a conscious grammar at all, and are apparently immune to the effects of correction." Such a person "relies mostly on his 'feel' for correctness." Other people, however, "monitor" their language use "all the time, and as a result exhibit little fluency" (1978, 10).

Children with learning disabilities might be seen as pronounced examples of individual differences. Normal children are able to use more than one strategy as the situation warrants: Thus Minh seemed to use a Gestalt strategy of picking up long chunks for Expressive speech situations and an Analytic strategy of picking up single words for Referential ones (Peters 1977). Children with learning disabilities differ from "normal" children, not in having access to totally different strategies, but rather in the relative degree to which they can use the same strategies. In particular, certain strategies may be all but denied to certain children. Weeks (1974) describes in detail a child who seemed to have limited access to certain strategies for language learning but who compensated by making fuller use of other strategies.

Of course, not all children with language-related learning disabilities are deficient in the same processing strategies. One suggestive study of dyslexic children found that they could be classed in several distinct subgroups, two of which were labeled "dysphonetic" and "dyseidetic" (Fried et al. 1981). The dysphonetic children "have great difficulty in reading and spelling words phonetically, though they may have a limited sight vocabulary of whole words which they can recognize and read fluently on flash presentation" (15). Dyseidetic children "read laboriously through a process of phonetic analysis and synthesis" (i.e., sounding out words letter by letter), and "they have a poor memory for visual whole-word and letter Gestalts," which leads to "difficulty recognizing words or . . . learning what letters look like" (15). Electroencephalographic measurements revealed neurological processing differences between the two groups. It would seem therefore that for neurological reasons dysphonetic children would have limited or no access to analytic strategies for processing print, whereas dyseidetic children would be unable to make much use of Gestalt strategies. Although these data concern reading, a parallel set of differences may exist for extractive processing of spoken speech.

The existence of large individual neurological differences among adults is consistent with the anatomical evidence summarized in Whitaker and Selnes (1976). For instance, a *fourfold* difference in the size of the area of the brain that processes visual stimuli has been observed among patients for whom this has been mapped (847), and large individual differences in the architecture of the receptive language areas have also been observed (848). Although some work has been done on interhemispheric asymmetries within infants (e.g., Chi, Dooling, & Gilles 1977; Wada, Clark, & Hamm 1975; Witelson & Pallie 1973), little is known about individual anatomical differences across infants. The potential importance of such differences has been acknowledged by Geschwind, who writes, "I have heard it said that the development of language is remarkably uniform across children. I am sure that there are major uniformities, but I suspect that there are many variations on this basic pattern, *determined by individual differences in organization of the brain*" (1980, 306, emphasis mine). If such anatomical differences can indeed be demonstrated among infants, this would constitute further evidence for variable inborn influences on early language-acquisition strategies.

These four factors – perception of language function, type of input, type of speech expected, and individual differences – may explain many of the observed strategy differences among children learning their first language. If we examine the diversity in these factors it does not appear remarkable that unit sizes differ and that one child should tend to isolate phrases while another is prone to isolate labels. Our duty as linguists, however, is not to select our data fastidiously from this variation but to develop and use the entire range as evidence for language-acquisition processes.

3   The segmentation of extracted units

According to the present view, after a number of units have been extracted and memorized, knowledge about them can be put to use in acquiring further knowledge about the language. In this chapter I will first consider what strategies might be used to refine and extend linguistic knowledge in two ways: the segmentation of extracted units into smaller units, and the perception of the structural patterns implied by these segmentations. I will then return briefly to the question of developmental variability and its possible causes.

3.1. Segmentation of units into smaller ones

In order to be able to progress beyond the mere recognition and production of single extracted units, the child needs to make a basic assumption, namely, that any such unit is potentially complex: that it may in turn be composed of smaller units that can be segmented out and stored independently. Once such an assumption has been made (or once that fact about language has been realized), the following general strategy can be applied:

SEGMENT.   Attempt to segment units into smaller ones and store these also as units.

It must be noted here that the discovery of certain kinds of morphological and syntactic patterns can be expected to follow hard on the heels of such segmentation; in fact, these two processes are inextricable. For ease of exposition, however, I will here consider them separately, deferring a discussion of pattern perception until 3.2.

It should also be noted that a unit, once segmented into smaller units, may not be forgotten but may remain available as a single unit for production purposes and for possible reanalysis in those cases where it is discovered that the first segmentation is erroneous. Some evidence for this sort of lexical redundancy will be examined in the next chapter.

3.1.1. Segmentation: internal cues

In order to segment a unit into smaller ones the child needs some heuristics for finding points at which to make cuts. Certain kinds of phonological salience can be expected to play a role here, highlighting either likely cut points (SG:RHYTHM and SG:INTONATION) or likely chunks to cut off (SG:END, SG:BEGIN, SG:STRESS, SG: REPETITION):

SG:END.   Segment off the last syllable of a unit from the rest.*

SG:BEGIN.   Segment off the first syllable of a unit from the rest.*

SG:STRESS.   Segment off a stressed syllable from the rest.

SG:RHYTHM.   Segment units at rhythmically salient places.*

SG:INTONATION.   Segment units at intonationally salient places.*

SG:REPETITION.   Segment off sub-units that are repeated (in segmentals or meter or melody) within the same unit.[8]

The syllables at the ends (SG:END) and beginnings (SG:BEGIN) of utterances have particular phonological salience, since they are adjacent to silence (EX:SILENCE). The ability to remember such syllables may be enhanced by the tendency for items at the end and beginning of a series (especially at the end) to be remembered better than items located in the middle (see Kintsch 1977 for a review of research on serial recall by adults, and Hagen & Stanovich 1977 for work with children).

In his study of the acquisition of Quiche Mayan, Pye (1980, 1981) makes a good case for the perceptual salience of word-final syllables, especially when they are stressed (SG:END and SG:STRESS). Note, however, that a strategy of paying attention to unit-final syllables (SG:END) would find less support in a language with word-initial stress. Such a situation would produce a conflict between two saliency factors: stress and recency. In such a case it would seem that the regularity of patterning of word-initial stress would override – at least once such regularity was perceived – that is, SG:STRESS and SG:BEGIN together would carry more weight than SG:END by itself.

Weir observed that her son Anthony oversegmented the two words *whistle* and *measure:* "The child owned a whistle and apparently did not like to use the same phonetic sequence for noun and verb, and the action of whistling he termed [wɪs]. The same apocopation was performed on *measure* where the verb became [mɛž]" (1962, 74). In both these cases Anthony seems to have segmented off the stressed syllables (which also happen to be the first syllables

---

[8] All of the heuristics flagged with an asterisk are adaptations of Operating Principles for the acquisition of syntax originally proposed by Slobin (1973, 1981). Many of the other heuristics presented in this chapter owe much to discussions with Slobin and his students in a seminar held at the University of California at Berkeley during the winter quarter, 1981.

of their respective adult words (SG:STRESS and SG:BEGIN)). Whether he was also invoking a noun:verb analogy such as *helper:help = measure:mezh* is hard to say. The possibilities for such analogies will be discussed later.

SG:RHYTHM and SG:INTONATION have been included by analogy with the corresponding extraction heuristics. I do not have evidence for the operation of either one without the support of other segmentation heuristics, and yet it seems reasonable that rhythm and intonation should play a part in determining segmentation points. It is most likely that their effect is a reinforcing one; see the discussion of convergence in 3.1.3.

SG:REPETITION is based on the fact that repetition of elements can increase their salience enough to overcome natural loss of accessibility owing to memory overload. Languages where SG:REPETITION would prove useful are those in which gender or number agreement is marked with phonologically repetitive morphemes. Thus, in Hebrew, plurality is marked on both noun and modifying adjective by suffixation of *-im* (masc.) or *-ot* (fem.), for example:

ha-yelad-*im*   ha-gdol-*im*   me-dabr-*im*   'The big boys speak'.
the boy   m. pl. the big   m. pl. speak   m. pl.   [Berman 1981b, 26]

Here the rhyming recurrence of *-im* may help the child to segment it.

In Bantu languages gender-class agreement is marked on both noun and modifying adjective (as well as on the verb if the noun in question is the subject of the verb) by prefixation of phonologically repetitive classifier particles. Two examples from Xhosa illustrate the alliterative quality of such repeated morphemes (cl = classifier):

b- onke a-*ba-* ntu *ba-* funa u- xolo   'All people want peace'.
cl. all   cl.   man cl.   want cl. peace

s- onke i-*si-* zwe   *s i* -funa u- xolo   'The whole nation wants peace'.
cl. all   cl.   nation cl.   want cl. peace   [Jordan 1966, 24]

3.1.2. *Segmentation: comparative method*

Another kind of phonological salience results from phonological similarity between two or more known units. This suggests a comparative heuristic, here stated in two parts, the second being a generalization of the first:

SG:MATCH1.   If the beginning or final portion of a unit is phonologically similar to another unit, the remainder of the larger unit is a candidate for storage as a unit.

SG:MATCH2.   More generally, if two units share *any* phonologically similar portion, the shared portion can be segmented out and stored as a unit, and so can the residues.

SG:MATCH1 is a relatively simply heuristic that segments an utterance into exactly two pieces, one of which is "known" and one of which may not be known. As children's linguistic knowledge and processing capacity grow they will be able to handle segmentations into more than two units. This generalization is expressed in SG:MATCH2 and will be considered in more detail later. For now I will confine the discussion to two-unit segmentations.

When making phonological comparisons such as those described in the MATCH heuristics, the child may draw the material to be compared from two sources: previously extracted and memorized speech (units in long-term memory) or more recently heard speech (units in short-term memory). Any combination of sources is presumed to be possible: Either the shorter unit or the longer unit in the match may be drawn from either long-term or short-term memory. If both units have just been heard in the input speech (e.g., the child's mother says, "See the tree? The tree"), segmentation may take place right away ("on line," to use a computer metaphor). If the longer unit has been memorized, either hearing one of its sub-units or somehow recalling it may trigger segmentation.

Evidence of such "off-line" processing might be gathered under circumstances in which children are obliging enough to play with their language aloud, as in the presleep monologues studied by Weir. Since Anthony Weir was 2;4 to 2;6 at the time of this study, he was largely beyond the early segmentation phase of language acquisition, although the following sequences are suggestive:

that's the right way
          right way   [1962, 164]
now the blanket's allgone
     the blanket's allgone
yellow blanket's allgone   [207]

I will call this segmentation process "fission," after Bateson: "When internal differentiation is made within a praxon [i.e., a unit that has already been acquired and used as a whole], as in the case of a child, competence is also being changed, by praxonic Fission" (1975, 62).

The effects of applying a heuristic such as SG:MATCH1 are most easily seen when children go too far and oversegment adult words. For instance, the word *behave* seems prone to such overanalysis by children learning English. Assuming that admonitions such as "I want you to be good" and "I want you to behave" are frequently heard, such a segmentation principle could be the basis of productions such as Rachel Scollon's "I'm going to be very very /heyv/," or Norman Gibson's "Daddy, Laura's not being /heyv/."[9]

The existence of sub-units that can occur in different orders can also lead to

---

[9] I have collected anecdotes on overanalysis of this particular word by four different children. The information has come from Robert Gibson, Michael Peters, Steven Schoen, and Ron Scollon.

matching and segmentation. Thus the realization that both "put your shoes on" and "put on your shoes" can occur would prevent both *shoes on* and *put on* from being fossilized as units.

Older children have also been observed to use a strategy of segmenting an unfamiliar long unit on the basis of a partial match with a familiar word. Thus, at age 4;0, when Kelly Horgan's mother "explained that Bonnie and Kathy lived in the same dormitory . . . Kelly asked: 'Is the mitory for Bonnie's door or Kathy's door?'" (Horgan 1980, 16).

Wong Fillmore (1976, 1979) shows that for her second-language learners English phrases that had been memorized and used as wholes were more easily segmented than constructions heard for the first time. Having the phrases constantly available in memory and knowing at least their holistic meanings meant that

the formulas the children learned and used constituted the linguistic material on which a large part of the analytical activities involved in language learning could be carried out . . . Once in the learner's speech repertory, they became familiar, and therefore could be compared with other utterances in the repertory as well as with those produced by other speakers . . . They provided the data on which the children were to perform their analytical activities in figuring out the structure of the language. [1979, 212]

Thus the formulas that these children found useful right from the beginning and that they originally assimilated whole so as to have something to say in a socially demanding play situation were also used by them as the basis for much of their linguistic analysis.

Roger Brown has described from a subjective point of view an experience with fission that he had when learning Japanese by the Berlitz method:

Hearing again and again the question *Kore wa nan desu ka?* (What is this?) but never seeing it printed I conceived of *korewa* as a single word; it is spoken without pause. Some lessons later I learned that *wa* is a particle, an unchanging uninflected form, that marks the noun it follows as the topic of the sentence. Interestingly enough I did not, at once, reanalyze my word *korewa* and such others as *sorewa* and *arewa* into noun and particle forms. I did not do that until I started to hear such object forms as *kore o* and *sore o* and *are o* in which *o* marks the direct object. Then the truth dawned on me, and the words almost audibly cracked into *kore, sore,* and *are,* three demonstratives which took *wa* in the nominative form and *o* in the objective. [1973, 5]

This observation provides support for the claim that speech that is originally learned in "long units" does not just fade away, but may provide material for eventual analysis, with the resulting pieces themselves becoming part of the growing language system.

The idea that memorized chunks can provide the raw material for much of a language learner's linguistic analysis has so far been explicitly proposed and explored by only a very few people. Wong Fillmore (1976, 1979), of course, is one of these. Another is Clark (1974, 1977), who considers the effects of her own two children's strategy of incorporating large chunks of preceding adult utterances into their own utterances, for example:

(4) Mother: We're all very mucky.

    Child: I   all very mucky too.

(5) Mother: Do you want to get off? (He was riding on a roundabout.)

    Child: No, I   want to get on. (Meaning, apparently, that he wanted to stay

                        on.)   [1974, 3, spacing mine]

In her 1977 paper she calls this strategy of copying a part of an adult utterance Extraction (342) and suggests that, armed with evidence that children do indeed do this, we reconsider

> Brown's (1968) examples of children's questions that he considers could not originate as imitations: *What he wants?, Why you can't open it?, What his name is?* Although these questions do not reflect the word order of well-formed adult questions, they do reflect the word order of well-formed adult dependent questions, i.e. *Ask him <u>what he wants</u>, He'll tell you <u>what his name is</u>.* Such dependent questions are very likely to be noticed by children, since they are common as answers to the child's own questions, e.g. Child: *Where teddy?* Mother: *I don't known where teddy is.* When is a child more likely to be attentive to what his mother has to say than when he has just asked her a question? The above response to *Where teddy?* could be interpreted by the child as an expansion which corrects the incomplete form of his own question. [1977, 343]

Later in the same paper she proposes that "imitation has a . . . positive role to play in the acquisition of syntax, by making adult forms available to the child, thus helping him to notice these forms more readily when adults use them, and enabling him to assimilate their function gradually through use" (351).

    Bolinger, too, suggests that "learning goes on constantly – but especially with young children – in segments of collocation size as much as it does in segments of word size, and that much if not most of our later manipulative grasp of words is by way of analysis of collocations" (1976, 8). Elsewhere he observes that

> words as we understand them are not the only elements that have a more or less fixed correlation with meaning. They are not even necessarily the first units that a child learns to imbue with this association. In the beginning stages a child apprehends holistically: the situation is not broken down, and neither is the verbal expression that accompanies it. That is why the first learning is holophrastic: each word is an utterance, each utterance is an undivided word, as far as the child is concerned. It is only later that words are differentiated out of larger wholes. [1975, 100][10]

---

[10] Note that Bolinger uses the term "holophrastic" in the less common perceptual sense of a single unit in the child's linguistic system made up of one or more morphemes of the adult language, rather than in the more common productive sense of a single word that is used as if it meant a whole sentence.

More recently, Snow has begun to look at the phenomenon of imitation more carefully. She points out that two specific kinds of imitation, both of which have generally been ignored for methodological reasons, may be particularly important windows on language development – namely, expanded and deferred imitations. Expanded imitations are defined as "including at least one stressed content word from the adult utterance and at least one word or morpheme not in the modelled utterance" (1981a, 207), for example,

Mother: What did we crash into last night, Nathaniel?
Nathaniel: Crash into living room.   [207]

Deferred imitations are those in which the copied, extracted, or imitated chunk does not get produced by the child right away, but only sometime later. Both Snow (1981a, 1981b) and Moerk and Moerk (1979) are able to show how such deferred or delayed imitations are used by their two subjects in developmentally progressive ways. Snow concludes that

the judicious use of expanded and deferred imitations on the part of a language learner might constitute a very effective strategy for performing communicatively far above his linguistic level, and might at the same time provide the learner with linguistic material which is susceptible to segmentation and further analysis. [1981a, 211]

3.1.3. Segmentation: evaluation

Not all applications of these segmentation heuristics just given will yield useful sub-units. In fact, most will not. Thus some heuristics are needed for evaluating possible segmentations, confirming some of them and being neutral about or disconfirming others. The three evaluation heuristics proposed here are based on three types of perceptual salience with respect to potential results of segmentation: convergence of several segmentation heuristics, frequency of resulting sub-units, and transparency of meaning:

EVAL:CONVERGE.   If several segmentation heuristics result in the same cut or sub-unit, the result is a better one than if only one segmentation heuristic could have achieved it.

EVAL:FREQUENCY.   If a particular sub-unit resulting from a segmentation occurs frequently, especially over a short span of time, it is better than one that occurs less frequently.

EVAL:MEANING.   If a clear meaning can be associated with a particular sub-unit resulting from a segmentation, then the cut is better than one that does not result in a unit with a clear meaning.

As with the extraction process, saliency factors can mutually reinforce each other, since if more than one is relevant their combination will increase the salience of a particular sub-unit. On the other hand, they may also work at cross-purposes, scattering different kinds of segmentation cues across an utterance. These different kinds of interaction possibilities are reflected in EVAL:CONVERGE.

Pye (1980, 1981) has shown for children learning Quiche Mayan that stress is a particularly important perceptual determinant of which (phonological) parts of morphologically complex words are acquired first. Moreover, SG:STRESS works particularly well in languages where stress is fixed with respect to word boundaries: In such languages children rarely make segmentation errors that cross word boundaries. Evidence for this conclusion comes from studies of the acquisition of languages such as Hungarian (MacWhinney 1974), which has word-initial stress, as well as Quiche, which has word-final stress and in which SG:STRESS can converge with SG:BEGIN or SG:END, respectively (EVAL:CONVERGE). (See Peters 1981 for further discussion.)

The application of EVAL:FREQUENCY may cause the persistence of many of the missegmentations that language learners make. An example of such a missegmentation in English is the overanalysis of *behave* through the false segmentation of *be*. Similar missegmentation errors, this time involving the more familiar forms of the definite article, occur in French acquisition; for example, *l'avion* may be perceived as *la vion*, *l'électricité* as *les lectricités*.[11]

As the child's linguistic system develops, awareness of her or his own speech may become an increasing source of saliency for (re)analysis and segmentation. As will be discussed in more detail shortly, segmentation results not only in subunits to be stored in the lexicon, but also in patterns for the formation of novel utterances, some of which may prove more acceptable than others. This suggests another evaluation heuristic:[12]

EVAL:PRODUCE.   If a novel utterance based on a presumed segmentation is not acceptable (not understood, not heeded, or somehow sounds funny), then such negative feedback casts suspicion on the segmentation.

It must be borne in mind, however, that although language learners must monitor their own speech and become aware of discrepancies between what they produce and what they hear, not all such discrepancies are equally accessible at a given stage of language development. This claim is attested by the oft-repeated anecdotes of children whose language is impervious to repeated corrections by adult caretakers (e.g., Braine 1971, 160–1). I would like to suggest that the monitoring and awareness of discrepancy that does take place occurs at those points in the system that are currently being most clearly focused on, since this is where the most active development is taking

---

[11] Eve Clark, personal communication.
[12] See also MacWhinney (1978) for discussion of a production–perception feedback cycle.

place. Any discrepancies that occur in the fuzzy background of detail not yet focused on will be ignored.

A segmentation that is rejected by these evaluation heuristics may simply be quietly forgotten (i.e., the sub-units may fade from storage), or it may be actively repaired.

SG:REANALYZE. When a segmentation fares poorly with respect to these evaluation heuristics, reanalyze the original unit.

The following sequence, reported to me by Steven Schoen, is a good example of SG:REANALYZE in action:

Christine is a 4-year-old girl; Steven is an adult male. They are riding in the back seat of a car. Christine is acting rowdy. Steven tells Christine she "must behave" if she wants Steven to read her a book. He is, however, paying more attention to a cassette tape that is playing music than he is to Christine. A couple of minutes later:

> C: Steven I am /heyv/.
> S: What? You hate? What do you hate?
> C: /heyv/. I am /heyv/.
> S: You hate? You hate me? The music? What?
> C: No, I am /heyv/. /heyv/.
> S: I don't know what you are talking about.

Silence. A bit later:

> C: I /heyv/.
> S: You hate me?
> C: (shakes her head no)
> S: Who do you hate?

Silence. A bit later:

> C: I am behaving.

In this example, Steven's repeated lack of understanding twice forced Christine to try and reanalyze the word *behave*. It was only when she reached the correct (adult) analysis that Steven became aware of the nature of her difficulty.

A somewhat more complex example of reanalysis comes from Iwamura's study of the speech of two 3-year-old girls, Suzy and Nani, who were recorded daily (five days a week) as they talked to each other in the back seat of a car on their way to or from nursery school. In order better to communicate with each other the girls often struggled valiantly with constructing a particular sentence, and in the process they sometimes produced evidence about analysis in progress. A particularly intriguing example involves what Iwamura calls the "unpacking" of the catenative *wanna*. In this instance Suzy (3;8) had suggested that Nani (3;5) pretend that Nani's shawl was a poncho, but Nani did not want to do this:

7.   S: Just pre*tend* to have a poncho.
8.   N: No, I wan' to. No I don' wanna. I wanna be it, a, shawl.
9.   S: Sha'
10.   N: I wan' it to be a *shawl*. I wa ⎰ n'
11.   S: ⎱ Sha', sha'
12.   N: (shouts) No, I say it my*self*. (giggles)   [1980, 85]

The reanalysis that allowed Nani to break *wanna* into *want to* so that she could insert *it* (line 10) can be seen more clearly if we look at the way Iwamura has diagrammed utterances 8–10:

8 N: No I	wan to	
8′ No I don	wanna	
8″ I	wanna be it,	a shawl.
9 S:		sha'
10 N: I	wan it to be	a shawl. [86]

As Iwamura points out, *wanna* is hard to analyze, not only because it tends to occur as a unit in American English, but also because it can be analyzed in two ways:

In the case of *wanna*, Nani had probably used it for a long time in sentences such as "I wanna cookie." and "I wanna come too." She would have had to learn the difference between *wanna* meaning "want a" and *wanna* meaning "want to" before she could approach the construction of *want* + NP + VP. [87]

Though it is a good bet that attention to catenatives such as *wanna, gonna, oughta,* and *hafta* will provide valuable insights into the fission process, Iwamura points out that evidence for this kind of analysis will have to be collected in conversational contexts. This is not only so that the successive breakdown stages can be observed, but also because such analysis tended to occur

at times when the children were under communicative stress. In such situations they felt an urgent need to express certain ideas. This need forced them to strain their linguistic resources to their current limits . . . The development of new analyses may occur at such moments of great communicative need. This is likely to be indicated by the breaking down of previously unanalyzed speech formulas. [1979, 10–11]

See 4.3 for further discussion of communication pressure.

3.2.   Extraction of morpho-syntactic frames

As I have already suggested, the process of segmenting units yields not only the sub-units but also information about the underlying structural pattern of the original unit. We are now ready to consider how children may extract and make use of such structural patterns.[13]

At the very early stages of acquisition of syntax that I discuss in this book, I do not believe that it is possible to distinguish between surface and deep linguistic structure with respect to children's internal representations of the simple morpho-syntactic frames[14] they are working with. Whether children go on to develop such a distinction, and if so how this might happen, is a question I am not prepared to address. Therefore my presentation here will be very much at the surface level.

Structural information does not become available to the learner immediately upon segmentation of a long unit into two shorter units through the application of SG:MATCH; at first the learner will know no more than that she or he is dealing with the juxtaposition of two units. If, however, the child is able to collect a number of segmented sequences, all of which begin (or end) with the same unit (e.g., *all clean, all done, all dry, all gone, all through, all wet*), she or he will be in a position to make an abstraction from unit + unit to unit + list (i.e., *all + clean, done, gone, through, wet*). As long as the list is a closed class of specific items where each combination has been learned individually, the pattern is not yet "productive," but is what Braine calls a "positional associative pattern" (1976, 9). (The example just given is from his data, p. 7.) The next move involves perhaps the most crucial abstraction in the early acquisition of syntax, the generalization from unit + (closed) list to unit plus (open) class. This move entails the recognition that there is some general feature that characterizes all the members of the list and that any other unit that shares this characterization can also be combined with this particular (constant) unit. Once this abstraction has been accomplished, the

---

[13] As we know, children do succeed in acquiring the syntax of adult language, by whatever means. In fact, they may be more successful at extracting patterned regularities from input language than are adult language learners (Newport 1981). We can speculate that although the apes that have been taught sign language may be able to extract units from the sign language they see, and although they might even be able to segment longer units into sub-units, it is precisely in the task of extracting the underlying structural patterns of these longer units that they may fail. As we shall see, there is evidence that such pattern extraction is at least one route to the acquisition of syntax for children. It would be of interest to look at the data on apes' acquisition of sign language within this framework to see how far they seem to be able to get, thus pinpointing their limitations more precisely.

[14] My term "morpho-syntactic frame" is approximately equivalent to Braine's (1976) term "positional formula" and Wong Fillmore's (1976) term "sentence frame." Braine and Wong Fillmore, however, are focusing on the productive aspects of early constructions, whereas I am focusing on the perception of constructional patterns, in particular, on awareness of constraints on the order of constituents (syntax), on the separation of content items from grammatical functors (morphology), and on the specification of possible slot fillers.

child has what Braine calls a "positional productive pattern" (1976, 8) and what Wong Fillmore calls a "frame" with an "analyzed slot" (1976, chap. 6). Although I will generally stick with Wong Fillmore's terminology, I may sometimes refer to such a pattern as being of the "constant + variable" type.

3.2.1. Frames

The move from unit + unit through unit + list to frame + slot is summarized in the following pair of heuristics:

FRAME.   If two (or more) units, after segmentation by any of the SG: heuristics, appear to share a common sub-unit, A, followed or preceded by alternative sub-units, B or C, and so on, take note of this fact, namely, that there is a pattern in which A can be followed (or preceded) by either B or C, and so on.

SLOT.   When you have a list of items, such as B, C, and so on, that can co-occur with a given unit, A, notice properties common to the members of the list and assume that other items that have those properties can also occur in that slot.

If the child assumes that such frames, which have been generalized from repeated instances of particular constructions, will continue to recur, the child can use this knowledge as a segmentation aid:

FR:SEGMENT.   Use known frames as templates in attempting to segment new utterances.

Although frames are different from lexical units in that they contain a variable part, they are a possible way to generalize units. That is, they could be viewed as a more general kind of unit, namely, one that has a variable part. Pursuing this line of inference could lead the child (or us) to a lexically based (theory of) syntax in which syntactic information is naturally stored in the lexicon. In any case, the main point here is that these frames, wherever they are stored, embody rudimentary syntactic information and represent a possible start in the learning of syntax.

Supporting data for this claim come from Braine's monograph (1976), in which he examines the data on the first word combinations of twelve children, looking for the kinds of early patterns they use. If, within a given child's corpus, there is a set of utterances involving combinations with a particular (constant) word (e.g., *more*), this is a "pattern." If there are statistically significantly more utterances with the constant term in one position than in the other, then the pattern qualifies as a "positional pattern" (11–12), for example, *more car, more cereal, more cookie, more fish, more hot, more juice, outside more* (7). (Required ratios for the .05 significance level include 6:0, 8:1, 9:2.) If all the combinations within a corpus could have been taken directly from adult utterances, the pattern is termed "positional associative" (9), for example, *more cereal, more fish, more juice*. If, however, there is evidence of novel combinations on the child's part, the pattern is considered to be "productive," for example, *more car* 'drive around some more', *more hot* 'another hot thing' (8).

Braine finds evidence in all twelve corpora for positional productive patterns. These patterns are, moreover, quite restricted semantically in that they are "formulae of limited scope for realizing specific kinds of meanings" (4). On the basis of semantic content he identifies a number of basic types of common early patterns, some of which are of the constant + variable type (the others will be dealt with in 3.2.3.), for example, *see* + X, *hot* + X, *two* + X, *more* + X, *allgone* + X, *there* + X, *want* + X (56–7). Although Braine's focus is on the limited semantic scope of these patterns, his data can be interpreted in terms of the limitations on combinatorial possibilities as well; that is, children learn a number of highly restricted two-part frames without perceiving for some time that they can be generalized into a smaller number of more general frames. Thus *big* + X, *little* + X, *hurt* + X, *old* + X would exist at first as independent frames rather than as a more general frame PROPERTY + X (33–5).

We will consider these more general frames presently; let us first examine some examples of two-part frames with one constant and one variable part. The oversegmentation of *behave* may in fact be based on the perception of a frame-and-slot type pattern since children are frequently exhorted to "Be good," "Be nice," or "Be quiet," as well as to "Behave." This could lead to the analysis Be X, where X = (*good, nice, quiet, /heyv/*).

As discussed in 2.2.2, for some children the input speech may include many expressions that introduce various kinds of labels. From such expressions these children may discover useful formulaic frames such as *that's a* X, *what's this* X, *see the* X, which can be used as segmentation aids. In fact, such a strategy may work so well that adult observers never notice it. But it could also lead to undersegmentations, as in the following examples:

1.   Clark (1977, 350; Adam nearly 2;4):

Mother: What's the cat's name?
 Adam: Cat name.
Mother: What's that a picture of?
 Adam: Picture of.

2.   Peters (tape of Minh at 1;9):

Mother: What is this whole thing?
 Minh: Whole thing.
Mother: Huh?
 Minh: Whole thing.

In these examples Adam and Minh seem to have been segmenting on the basis of frames such as <u>*what's the*</u> X, <u>*what's that a*</u> X, and <u>*what's this*</u> X. Or perhaps they had discovered only a single poorly perceived frame such as <u>*what's th*</u>—— X.

A similar strategy can be used in Hebrew, where labels are introduced by the morpheme *ze*, as in *ze kelev* 'This/ it's a dog'. Ruth Berman has described for me a three-year-old Israeli child who talked about an animal called a *bra* for which no one could determine the referent. Finally they realized that she was referring to a zebra: *zebra* had been heard as *ze bra* 'It (is a) *bra*'.

Thomas (1980) describes the speech of fathers to their 2-year-old sons as they were videotaped in a laboratory playroom. She finds that much of this speech can be described in terms of routines that have predictable associations between syntactic forms and pragmatic functions; in fact, she calls them "SYN-PRAG" routines. These include not only noun and attribute introducers such as *that's(-a)* X, but also such verb introducers as

   whyncha + verb (why don't you X)
      let's + verb
  wammeda + verb (want me to X)
    can you + verb
    ya hafta + verb

Perception of such frames could help these boys to segment labels for actions (i.e., verbs).

In her study of Spanish-speaking children learning English, Wong Fillmore discusses what she calls "sentence producing tactics." She notes that these sometimes involve "paradigmatic substitution" in "formulaic sentence frames" where substitution slots have been discovered but the syntax of the whole construction has not yet been completely analyzed (1976, 305).

Consider, for example, *I wanna X*, where *X* is a *NP*, which functioned as a formulaic sentence frame for some of the children. The use of the categorial symbol *NP* indicates that in this particular formula, the structure has been analyzed to the extent that the user realizes that a variety of noun phrases can be substituted in the formulaic frame, such as "I wanna *the little ones toys*," "I wanna *red color*," and "I wanna *you toy*." The NP's themselves may or may not be analyzed further – that is, some may be analyzed into component parts . . . or they may be partially or wholly unanalyzed formulas themselves. [306]

At least three of the children whom Wong Fillmore studied were observed to go through a stage where they were producing utterances consisting of either one or two units, and many of these two-unit utterances were based on formulaic frames. Thus Juan during Time II[15] produced formulaic sentences built on <u>*I wanna be*</u> + noun phrase, for example, "I wanna be the doctor," "I

---

[15] Time I refers to the first quarter of the school year during which Wong Fillmore conducted the study; Time II is the second quarter.

wanna be the cowboy" (320–1). Similarly, Jesus during Time I produced for-mulaic sentences built on *lookit, looky,* or <u>*hey look*</u> + NP or adverb, for exam-ple, "lookit, like that," "looky, chicken" (344). And Alej during Time I produced three types of formulaic constructions: unit + vocative, for example, "'scuse me, Kevin," "Teacher, wha' happen?'"; formulaic sentences built on *looky* or *lookit* + X *see*, for example, "Looky telephone see," "Looky see"; formulaic sentences formed from NP + *es brokie*, for example, "Mi pencil es brokie" (374).

3.2.2. *Frames: evaluation*

As we have seen, even in this limited two-part form, frames can be useful in the segmentation process itself, in that, once a frame is established ("taken note of" in the terminology of FRAME), the occurrence in speech of the constant part of the frame can be a strong indication that an unfamiliar neighboring unit (preceding or following, as the case may be) is extractable, and thus that the whole construction is segmentable. This leads to a new evaluation heuristic based on the recognition of frames:

EVAL:FRAME. If a segmentation yields the form of a known frame, the segmenta-tion (and its sub-units) is probably a good one.

Just as with units, meaning may accrue to certain frames. There may be a convergence at work here in evaluating frames: If a frame can be clearly tied to some meaning, it is a better frame than one that cannot.

A frame may occur so frequently with unfamiliar slot fillers that children may come to expect a large class of units to occur in that frame. This could lead to a production strategy in which children produce not only utterances they have previously heard and extracted, but novel utterances based on such a frame, filling the slot with an item that they may never have heard in this slot but that shares some similarity with items they have heard there. This strategy can produce feedback for confirming or disconfirming the segmenta-tion of the frames themselves, in a manner analogous to EVAL:PRODUCE.

FR:EVAL.PRODUCE. Use the feedback from novel utterances based on a presumed frame to evaluate the frame.

When these evaluation heuristics converge with those suggested earlier, both the frame and the sub-units will be reinforced. Thus the overanalysis of *behave* may be reinforced by frequency as well as by the good fit to a familiar pattern – until attempts to make novel constructions with one of the sub-units result in negative feedback and force reanalysis.

Wong Fillmore's subject Nora was a child who was particularly willing to produce utterances using new frames she had discovered, discarding those that did not seem to work well and keeping those that did. For instance, she made use of the similarities and differences of two formulas that she had learned (*I wanna play wi' dese*, and *I don' wanna do dese*) to discover two frames. In Wong Fillmore's words:

> No doubt the similarity of these expressions allowed her to discover that the constituents following *wanna* were interchangeable, and that she could say *I don' wanna play wi' dese* and *I wanna do dese*. As soon as she realized that these phrases were interchangeable, she was on her way to discovering that similar phrases could be inserted. At that point, these formulas became formulaic frames with analyzed slots: *I wanna X* [where] $X = VP$ and *I don' wanna X* [where] $X = VP$. [1979, 212–13]

In terms of the heuristics presented here, we could say that Nora first used SG:MATCH to match up and segment the *wanna* in the two phrases that she had already extracted:

> I-wanna play-wi'-dese
> I-don'-wanna do-dese

Application of FRAME would then result in the two formulaic frames described by Wong Fillmore. Positive feedback from the production of the new constructions suggested by these frames would be evaluated by FR:EVAL.PRODUCE, and would result in confirmation of the segmentations, the resulting frames, and the sub-units.

But this is not the end of the story, since Nora went on to apply her heuristics to her new (sub-) unit *play wi' dese*, with further analysis resulting: When she realized that *dese* could be segmented from *play wi'* and replaced by any NP she had a new formulaic frame *play wi'* X, where X = NP. This formulaic frame could now be used wherever a verb phrase was called for, including, for example, *Le's* X, where X = VP ("Le's play wi' dese"). The breakdown process can be schematized as follows:

Utterance	*Analysis*
Iwannaplaywi'dese.	(unit)
Iwanna playwi'dese.	Iwanna + VP
playwi' dese	playwi' + NP

Wong Fillmore concludes:

> Thus, the analytical process carried out on formulas yielded formulaic frames with abstract slots representing constituent types which could substitute in them, and it also freed constituent parts of the formula to function in other constructions either as formulaic units or as wholly analyzed items. Finally, when all of the constituents of the formula have become freed from the original construction, what the learner has left is an abstract structure consisting of a pattern or rules by which he can construct like utterances. [1979, 213]

3.2.3. Frames: generalization

So far we have considered only how children might deal with simple two-part frames. It is possible to generalize such frames in several directions. I have already mentioned that children may generalize by inserting into the slot units they have never actually heard in that position. Moreover, the shape of the frame itself may become more complex. I will for convenience describe this development with the simplified statement:

FR:GENERALIZE.   Look for more general frames.

This heuristic produces several types of increasingly general results: discontinuous frames with one slot, discontinuous frames with multiple slots, and frames so general they can no longer be termed "frames."

Discontinuous frames with one slot.   Let us first look at some evidence that children are indeed able to handle discontinuous frames. Then we will consider the question of discontinuity more generally.

Sinikka Hayasaka observed that her son Satoshi, while at the stage where he was constructing utterances no longer than two words (1;8), learned the sentence *What a nice bicycle you have* from some Sony Talking Cards he had.[16] Soon after he learned this sentence he produced "What a nice elbow you have" and then "What a nice daddy you have." Assuming that Satoshi already knew the words *bicycle* and *daddy* (*elbow* appeared for the first time in this construction), we can say that after extracting *What a nice bicycle you have* he used the word *bicycle* and SG:MATCH2 to segment this phrase as follows:

what-a-nice bicycle you-have
            bicycle

By then applying FRAME he would have discovered the pattern

what-a-nice   X   you-have

which he then tried out (applying FR:PRODUCE), replacing X with other units he knew *(Daddy, elbow)* and evaluating the response (EVAL:PRODUCE). There is not enough evidence to determine just how general a pattern Satoshi was able to induce, although his mother noted that he used only concrete nouns in the phrase. He does, however, seem to have found a formulaic frame with an analyzed slot, much as Wong Fillmore's subjects did.

---

[16] Personal communication. These cards are designed for teaching English to Japanese speakers: A sentence is recorded on a magnetic tape strip along the card, and when the card is inserted in a special playback machine the recording is heard. Satoshi was able to operate the machine himself and loved to play with the cards.

Slobin (1973, 1981) and MacWhinney (1978) have repeatedly suggested that discontinuity is difficult for a child to deal with. Their evidence comes from certain discontinuous structures (e.g., French negative *ne . . . pas;* Arabic negative *ma- . . . -sh;* English progressive *be . . . -ing;* Russian and Hungarian case marking involving both prepositions and case suffixes), which children seem to deal with by first producing only the second of the two elements in question. Saliency factors surely play some role in the particular cases cited. Thus French *ne* is phonologically almost nonexistent. Is the same true for Arabic *ma-?* The English *-ing* suffix is certainly the most constant aspect of the progressive, since the form of the verb *be* not only is variable *(is, am, are)* but can be phonologically much reduced *('s, 'm, 're).* As for the case-marking constructions (e.g., Russian locative), it may be that the prepositions are more variable than the case inflections (i.e., that several different prepositions take the same inflection). If this is true then the more constant (or frequent) inflections would be more salient. Of course, the greater salience of word ends may have an effect here, too. In other words, the cited examples do not provide a real test of the effects of discontinuity, since the two pieces are not equally salient.

All of these cases, moreover, involve discontinuous *morphemes,* where the two pieces are at once semantically and functionally related. These relationships do not necessarily hold for discontinuous *frames.* Thus, although at the morphological level there may be justification for Slobin's "Avoid interruption . . . of linguistic units" (1973, 199) or MacWhinney's "The child avoids acquisition of discontinuous morphemes" (1978, 11), discontinuous frames do not need to be avoided altogether. Evidence from the success of pattern practice and substitution drills shows that adult language learners can handle discontinuous frames quite easily. And the example just cited of Satoshi Hayasaka shows that children can handle such frames, too.

On the other hand, Slobin's and MacWhinney's claims do reflect two common-sense processing constraints suggested by Slobin (1981); since it is hard to process too many elements at once one should do two things: attempt to keep the total number of elements in—any structure to a minimum, and try not to be processing more than one element at a time (i.e., one should at first proceed as if structures are not embedded). But if the situation seems to require it, discontinuity is acceptable (within one's processing capabilities).

Discontinuous frames with multiple slots.   Although I have no example of such frames from first-language acquisition, the following, from Wong Fillmore, is a good example from children's second-language acquisition and shows what we might expect to find in the former type of data. After around five months of exposure to English, 7-year-old Jesus had the following sentence frame:

is + Verb + *it* + Noun phrase

which led to such productions as

Is putting it dese.
Is making it the car.
Is got   it dese one.
Is got   it un truck.   [1976, 350]

A constant part of a frame becomes a variable.   Finally, the frame may itself "dissolve," the constant parts (or some of the constant parts) becoming variable slots. Ultimately the entire frame becomes a pattern of slots fillable by specific classes of items.

    Evidence for this step can be found in Braine (1976) and Ewing (1981). In 3.2.1 we saw that some of the basic types of common early patterns that Braine identifies are of the constant + variable type. The others are of the variable + variable type (X + Y) and express such basic semantic notions as possession 'X has a Y', class membership 'X is a Y', actor + action 'X Ys', and location 'X is in, on, or has moved to Y' (Braine 1976, 56–7). Working within Braine's concept of limited-scope patterns, Ewing asks how children might extend their productive capabilities. He proposes that in order to do so they would have to "integrate these patterns to create . . . more inclusive patterns" (2), and he suggests that there are two main kinds of pattern integration, "horizontal" and "vertical." We will discuss horizontal integration later in this section, under "Generalization of slots." Vertical integration involves just the kind of generalization of the constant parts of frames that we are concerned with here, for example,

$$\left. \begin{array}{c} \text{big/little} + \text{X} \\ \text{hot} + \text{X} \end{array} \right\rangle \quad \text{property} + \text{X}$$

Ewing shows how his data on the two- and three-word productions of five children are consistent with an integrative process in which patterns of the constant + variable type are generalized to the variable + variable (X + Y) type. For example, he demonstrates how utterances such as *I dining, I do, me walk, Guy play,* and the like generalize to Experiencer + Experience (5).

    Repeated finer and finer analysis of long chunks of language and concomitant generalization of the associated frames have been well documented for children acquiring second languages. The following example, from Wong Fillmore (1979, 213–5), shows four stages in such an iterative analysis by Nora:

1.   Two months of exposure to English. Nora's English productions included the unanalyzed unit:

      How do you do dese?

2.   Five months of exposure to English. Nora had extracted enough underlying structure from sentences containing this chunk to discover the following sentence pattern, which she used productively:

How do you do dese + X   where X could be a noun phrase or a prepositional phrase.

For example,
How-do-you-do-dese?
How-do-you-do-dese flower power?
How-do-you-do-dese in English?

She then used the language she heard or knew in order to segment *do dese* from *how do you*, and used the latter as the base for another productive sentence pattern:

$\left.\begin{array}{c}\textit{How do you}\\ \textit{How did you}\end{array}\right\}$ + X   where X could be a verb phrase.

For example,
How-do-you make the flower?
How-did-you make it?

3.   Seven months of exposure to English. Nora had segmented *you* off, and used the following sentence pattern:

$\left.\begin{array}{c}\textit{How do}\\ \textit{How does}\\ \textit{How did}\end{array}\right\}$ + X   where X could be a whole clause.

For example,
How-do   cut is?
How-does this color is?
How-did   dese work?   (= 'How does this work?')

4.   Sometime later *how* was also segmented off and used in constructing questions:

For example,
How you make it?
How will take off paste?

Thus, over a period of several months, Nora was able to analyze and then further analyze an extracted unit, discovering in the process a series of increasingly general frames that she then made use of productively.

Generalization of slots.   A different dimension of generalization of frames involves the evolution of a clearer perception of the properties of the slot fillers. There are two main ways to generalize slot fillers. One, which we have already seen in 3.2, involves noticing that the fillers of certain slots are always characterized by certain semantic properties, or come from a restricted (closed) class, or are constrained in some other way. The slots may thus become associated with such generalized properties or features or classes, rather than with actual lists of items. This is the move from constant + list to constant + class. Evidence that children do indeed generalize the properties of slots is found when they produce novel two-unit utterances consisting of an invariant linguistic chunk plus a variable part drawn from some semantic or other class, for example,

That's a + label
I'm unna + action

We have seen such generalizations in a number of the examples already cited in this chapter, for example, Satoshi's generalization of the *bicycle* slot to include *Daddy* and *elbow*; Jesus's action *(putting, making, got)* and object *(dese, the car, dese one, un truck)* slots; and Nora's more complex analysis and refinement.

A second approach to the generalization of slots involves the realization that slot fillers may themselves be frames. If it is true that frames are a possible generalization of units (as proposed in 3.2), it would follow that if units can occur in frames, frames must be able to do so too. [17] This type of generalization corresponds to Ewing's second kind of pattern integration, which he terms "horizontal" (1981, 3), for example,

$$\left.\begin{array}{c} \text{big/little} + \text{X} \\ \text{see} + \text{X} \end{array}\right> \quad \text{see} + \text{big/little} + \text{X}$$

$$\left.\begin{array}{c} \text{I} + \text{want} \\ \text{want} + \text{X} \end{array}\right> \quad \text{I} + \text{want} + \text{X}$$

Horizontal integration also involves the important move from two- to three-word utterances, and Ewing's data again support such a process.

3.3. Further examples

Let us now look at several more complex examples, each of which illustrates the application of several of the heuristics that we have been considering. The first two examples illustrate children's temporary misanalyses of bits of the language they are trying to learn – misanalyses that are eventually corrected. The subsequent examples are from older children and adults, and they illustrate how the use of certain heuristics can lead to misperceptions or misanalyses, some of which may persist for a long time.

1. The following data from Minh are rather intriguing because they seem to reveal a case of misanalysis that was temporarily reinforced by another (phonologically similar) word that happened to come along at just the crucial time. Briefly, the sequence (as I reconstruct it from my tapes and field notes [18]) was as follows: At 1;9 Minh was given a book containing a picture of

---

[17] I am indebted to Robert Hsu for this observation.

[18] Field notes, vol. 2, p. 69. Since I was out of town between 1;9 and 1;11 I am relying on what was told me by Minh's mother and Ron Scollon about developments while I was away.

a cow in a mid-leap over a crescent moon. This picture was accompanied by the phrase "The cow jumping over the moon." This seems to have fascinated him, and he evidently segmented off the first (stressed) and last syllables of this phrase, which he produced himself as "cow moon." This phrase was then extended to "cow moon daddy," which he was heard to repeat "at least fifty times" at a party one evening – whenever he saw either the moon or his daddy. At this point any reference to a cow already seems to have gotten lost.

The next development seems to have been that by 1;11 *cow,* which had the form ⟨ka⟩,[19] was interpreted as an existential demonstrative introducer for labels: He seems to have constructed a frame ⟨*ka*⟩ + X, where X was some kind of label. Thus my data include "ka moon," "ka baby," and "ka dirty." For the next month or so ⟨ka⟩ showed up sporadically in my tapes, especially when Minh was reading books and pointing out things, for example [ka lu] 'ka (ba)lloon', [ka mu] 'ka moon', [ka pipi] 'ka/gotta(?) peepee'. It was not, however, the only form used to introduce labels, since I also find ⟨ba⟩ (e.g., [ba bɛrz] 'the bears', [ba sak] 'the sock') and ⟨dɪ(z)⟩ (e.g., [dɪrai] 'this write', [dɪz xrak] 'this clock'). At 1;11.18 the use of ⟨ka⟩ increased slightly, at least on my tapes; it was now used to point out things he saw while watching television.

A week later (1;11.25) a new, and evidently temporarily confusing, element entered the picture in the form of his brother's new Kikaida doll.[20] In the tape I made on that day Minh said ⟨kadaw⟩ more than twenty times in referring to Kikaida doll. Although he made a few tries at a fuller pronunciation, for example, [kadhaida:], [haikədaw], he seems to have settled on ⟨kadaw⟩ as the best working version of *Kikaida* for the moment. Moreover, since he also heard the word *doll* in other combinations, he must have segmented ⟨kadaw⟩ into *ka doll* on the basis of his extracted and productive frame. Later on in the same tape, when he was watching "Sesame Street" with his brother, Minh used ⟨ka⟩ at least seventeen times in the old existential/demonstrative way as he commented about things he was seeing on the screen, for example, "ka lion," "ka four," "ka nine," "ka foot," "ka fall-down." Since I recorded the peak usage of the existential ⟨ka⟩ on the same day that Kikaida entered the picture, it seems as if the one temporarily reinforced the other. By the time of the next tape, two weeks later (2;0.9), the usage of ⟨ka⟩ seems to have been

---

[19] Since Minh's pronunciation often varied rather widely I have adopted the convention of using angle brackets in such cases to indicate a reconstructed underlying target form (an abstracted impressionistic average). In this case, ⟨ka⟩ varied phonetically from [ka] and [kə] (most of the time) to [kai] and [kəi] a few times.

[20] Kikaida is a Japanese superhero, the subject of a television series that was then the rage among children in Hawaii, who eagerly acquired all the toys that were being produced to take advantage of this enthusiasm.

restricted to reference to Kikaida, and this development was confirmed by his mother at 2;1.13.

This history of the evolution of ⟨ka⟩ is a good illustration of the complexity of the task of linguistic analysis that the child faces, as well as of the difficulty the linguist has in drawing inferences about what is going on. A good guess about the sequence of strategies applied by Minh is the following:

1. He uses SG:BEGIN, SG:STRESS, and SG:END to segment *cow* and *moon* from the beginning and end of "The cow jumping over the moon."
2. He produces them together and fuses them into a single phrase with the underlying pattern *ka + moon*.
3. He uses FRAME to generalize this pattern to a frame with a slot *ka + X*, where X is some kind of label.
4. He uses SG:MATCH1 and FR:SEGMENT to segment the new unit *Kikaida* into *ka + doll*, on the basis of this pattern and another known unit, *doll*.
5. He discovers through feedback and further analysis (EVAL:PRODUCE, SG:REANALYZE) that *ka* is not used in an existential/demonstrative way by adults. This leads to loss of *ka* except in referring to Kikaida. The existential/demonstrative function is taken over by ⟨dɪsɪz⟩ and ⟨dɪsə⟩.

2. Another insight into the segmentation process is drawn from data on 3- to 6-year-olds that were collected in Pasadena, California (Peters & Zaidel 1980). The subjects were thirty nursery school children, five boys and five girls from each of three classes (Group IV: range 5;1–6;3, mean 5;8; Group III: range 4;3–5;1, mean 4;10; and Group II: range 3;3–4;5, mean 3;10, Group I having been found incapable of performing the tasks in question). The tasks the children were asked to perform included a picture-naming one ("Can you show me X?") and a homonym-recognition one (presentation of four pictures together with the instruction "Can you show me two pictures that [have names that] sound the same but mean different kinds of things?")

One item in particular shows an interesting progression from an all but unknown vocabulary item in Group II, through a unitary item in Group III, to a segmented phrase in Group IV. This was the word *bow* as in <u>*bow and arrow.*</u> On the naming task ("Can you show me bow?"), only four of the ten children in Group II, when presented with four pictures including one of a bow and arrow but none with a ribbon-type bow, were able to point to the right picture (see Table 1). Of these four, two spontaneously made remarks as they pointed: "That's a bow an' arrow for the Indians," "Bow a' arrow." In Group III all of the children could point to the correct picture (although one needed a second try), and half of them made spontaneous remarks about "bow and arrow," including the phonological misanalyses "bow and narrow" and "bow nan arrow" ("bone an' arrow"?). In Group IV all but one did the naming task correctly, and only one asked "Bow an' arrow?"

Table 1. *Children's naming and homonym responses to* bow (and arrow)

Group	Naming		Homonyms1		Homonyms2		
	No. corr.	Spont. phrase	No. corr.	Spont. phrase	No. corr.	Confusion w. *bone*	Spont. phrase
II	4	2	3	1	1	2	1
III	9 > 10	5	4 > 6	3	1 > 6	4	2
IV	9	1	6 > 8	2	5 > 8	0	0

Note: > = after self-correction.

The homonym-recognition task was given twice: The first time the set of pictures was *bow* (ribbon), *bow* (and arrow), *gun*, *hoe* [rhyme]; the second time the pictures were *bow* (ribbon), *bow* (and arrow), *know*, *bone* [assonance]. The target pictures differed from the first set to the second. On the first presentation the homonyms were found by three children in Group II, six in Group III (of whom two made at least one wrong choice to begin with but clearly knew why the correct pair was right when they found it), and eight in Group IV (of whom, again, two self-corrected). Again several spontaneously said the phrase "bow an' arrow" while doing the task (see Table 1).

The second presentation of the homonym task was the more interesting for us in that it contained (by design) an assonance, *bone*, that (unintentionally) was phonologically contained in the phrase *bow and arrow*. And this phrase seems to have been the way the vocabulary item *bow* was first acquired by most of these children. The results on this presentation were slightly poorer than on the previous one (see Table 1): one correct in Group II, six in Group III (of which five made initial wrong choices), and eight in Group IV (of which three were initially wrong). When we look at the distribution of mistakes involving *bone* we find two in Group II (and in neither case is it clear that the phrase *bow and arrow* played any part) and none in Group IV. In Group III, however, four of the children picked *bone* as one of their choices, and two of them very clearly were confused by the phrase "bowan'arrow." For example, A.J., girl 5;1:

Points to	Says	Investigator says
knot, ribbon bow,	String and string.	That's the same kind of string. They should have different meanings.
bow and arrow	Bow an' arrow.	And?
bone	Bone.	Bow and bone?
	Nope. Bow an' arrows. Bow an' arrows an' bone.	They're not the same, are they?
	Bone. Bone an' bone.	

Another example is E.N., girl 4;3. She couldn't find the pair when asked to "find two that sound the same but mean different kinds of things," so the investigator (by design) pointed to the bow and arrow and asked if she could find "another picture that sounds like this."

Points to	Says	Investigator says
	Bone an' narrow?	
	I don' know where the other one.	
ribbon bow	Bone an' arrow	
bone	Bone an' arrow? Ah where dat other bone an' arrow?	Well, maybe not the whole thing.
	Bone. Bone an' arrow.	

In summary, then, these data seem to illustrate the following developmental sequence with respect to the word *bow*: The youngest children (Group II) tended not to know the word at all; when it was first learned (Group III) it tended to be learned as part of the unitary phrase <u>*bow and arrow*</u>, which may have been tied to a particular context ("for the Indians"). The Group IV children, however, had already correctly segmented *bow and arrow* into its adult constituents. The fact that five of the children in Group III who had difficulty with the homonym task in the presence of the distractor *bone* were eventually able to find the right pair seems to indicate that for these children the segmentation process may already have begun but had not yet been completed. That is, the data they had gathered so far on this phonological sequence were not yet sufficient to allow them to reject *bone* immediately as a possible candidate for a constituent. Once the learner feels confident in making such rejections categorical and immediate, segmentation can be said to be complete.

3.   Let us now turn to evidence for the use of segmentation heuristics by older language processors. In order to make sense of the streams of speech they hear, even adults must apply strategies such as those we have been discussing. Adults differ from children, however, in that their use of these strategies has become very automatic, and their knowledge of the potential words and structures they will hear is very extensive. Nonetheless, they may occasionally make wrong guesses about segmentation points or sub-units. If such guesses are too much at odds with the expected context of a message, an attempt at repair will be made. The following discussion is based on data from two of the few studies that have been made of such misperceptions (Browman 1978; Garnes & Bond 1980).

Browman (1978) deals with a corpus of 222 misperceptions that were heard to occur in casual speech. The errors were collected by linguists in Los Angeles, California, and Columbus, Ohio, who actually observed their occurrence. A careful look at Browman's data suggests that perceptual analysis of chunks of fluent speech follows a specific set of steps (in English, at least). Attention is first paid to those syllables with primary stresses (SG:STRESS). Since these are the most salient syllables, containing longer, fuller vowels, aspirated stops, and so on, they are more accurately perceived phonetically. Next an attempt is made to find a sequence of plausible lexical items[21] that fit with the stress pattern and the segmental sequences of the matched (stressed) syllables (SG:MATCH). The next step is to try to interpret the unstressed syllables in such a way that the syntactic expectations for the phrase are met without violating the rhythmic stress pattern of the input (FR:SEGMENT). It appears that in these unstressed syllables phonemes may be added, dropped, or altered as necessary to accomplish this syntactic-semantic fit. Also, contrary to Browman's claims about the phonetic saliency of word boundaries (96–7), these seem to get shifted quite often (e.g., in about one-third of the examples in Browman's corpus).

Garnes and Bond consider a corpus of approximately 900 errors collected in circumstances similar to Browman's. On the basis of their data they propose four basic (ordered) strategies for speech perception (1980, 237–8; I have embedded, in square brackets, the corresponding heuristics developed in this chapter):

1.   "Pay attention to stress and intonation patterns" (237) [SG:INTONATION, SG:RHYTHM, SG:STRESS] and segment the utterance into "phrases that can at least roughly be identified on the basis of stress and intonation" (238) [EX:SUPRASEG, EX:RHYTHM].

2.   "Pay attention to stressed vowels" (237) [SG:STRESS].

3.   "Find a word" (238); that is, scan for possible lexical items [SG:MATCH].

4.   "Find a phrase," which must "be given some semantic analysis, 'edited' for appropriate morphological markers, and probably ultimately unified into a semantic representation of the utterance" (238) [FR:SEGMENT, EVAL:FRAME].

If the listener cannot come up with an analysis that makes syntactic-semantic sense, the misperception will have to be signaled and the original utterance clarified. It is interesting to note, however, that in those errors that have been reported, syntactic integrity seems to take precedence over semantic plausibility. That is, when it is possible to make an analysis at all, the resulting phrase fits the preceding sentence syntactically, even though it may not fit semantically.[22]

Let us look at a specific example, one in which I was heard to say "in closeted time" when I had actually said "a clause at a time." The entire sentence was "Pawley thinks that people construct sentences *a clause at a*

---

[21] By "plausible" I mean that somehow they also fit in semantically with the listener's expectations.

[22] A. W. F. Huggins has pointed out to me, however, that this seeming bias may be due to the greater communicative need for reporting misperceptions that are semantic misfits than for reporting those that are syntactic misfits but make semantic sense.

time." My hearer evidently had no trouble identifying the stressed syllables [klaz] and [taim], although his semantic interpretation of the former was at variance with my intention. Next he had to account for three unstressed syllables, which he accomplished by adding two phonemes, altering an unstressed vowel, and deleting two word boundaries, to come up with an adverbial phrase that did not make sense – hence his request for repair:

a clause at a time: [ə k l á z ə t ə t à i m]
in closet-ed   time: [ɪ n k l á z ə t ə d t à i m]

Thus the kinds of extraction and segmentation heuristics that are crucial to children learning a new language system are useful, in a less major way, to adults in their processing of heard speech.

3.4. Factors affecting the course of segmentation

So far we have been focusing on children's heuristics for segmenting extracted units. Just as with the extraction process, however, the course of segmentation will depend not only on children's own processing activities but also on the kinds of data they have to work with and on the amount and type of cooperation they get from their caretakers. Therefore we also need to look at possible external and interactive influences on segmentation, considering in turn properties of input speech that may facilitate segmentation, the importance for segmentation of certain kinds of variation in the input, the possible contribution of interactive routines, and individual differences among children.

3.4.1. Input speech

In 2.2.2 we looked at ways in which input speech might affect the extraction process. Now let us consider what sorts of characteristics of the speech addressed to children may help or hinder children in applying particular segmentation strategies and in discovering adult sub-units and structural patterns in the speech they hear. For instance, bearing in mind heuristics such as SG:STRESS, SG:INTONATION, and SG:RHYTHM, we can ask whether caretakers add stresses to important words, use exaggerated and characteristic intonation or rhythmic contours with certain words or phrases, or prolong certain words or syllables. Any such modifications could serve to make it easier for the child to apply one or more segmentation heuristics. What is the evidence?

Garnica looked at prosodic and paralinguistic aspects of input, comparing the speech of middle-class English-speaking mothers to 2-year-olds, 5-year-olds, and adults. Some of the differences she found include more rising sentence-final pitch contours when addressing 2-year-olds (even on impera- tives, which normally have falling final contours); whispered *parts* of sen- tences in speech to 2-year-olds but not to older listeners; and addition of primary stresses resulting in more than one per sentence when addressing 2-year-olds (1977, 80–1). As Garnica points out, these modifications probably have general social and communicative effects in that they function to get the child's attention and to focus on the communicatively important aspects of adult utterances. But she also notes that they can serve to help the child perform linguistic analysis on the input. Thus she hypothesizes that the distinctive rising pitch terminals may help the child to locate sentence boundaries, since "the high pitch would tend to accentuate the termination of the sentence by the speaker" (84). Similarly, the addition of duration and stress to crucial content words would serve to "indicate to the child the 'key' words in the sentence" (84), not only enhancing commu- nication but also serving to indicate which sub-units should be extracted first. Moreover, the addition of extra primary stresses "may serve to divide up a sentence perceptually into smaller units. The adult thereby segments the sentence into pieces he/she thinks are of adequate size for the child to process easily . . . By this division, the adult may be providing the child with important information about constituent structure" (85). From Garnica's study, then, it is clear that at least in some cultures prosodic modifications of the input speech do occur along just those lines that would provide support for certain of the prosodically oriented heuristics.

3.4.2. *Variation in the input*

The most central of the proposed segmentation heuristics, however, is phonological matching (actually presented already as the two related heu- ristics SG:MATCH1 and SG:MATCH2, but collectively referred to as SG:MATCH). Let us see what sort of support for such a strategy may be present in input speech. If we look first at studies of middle-class English- speaking mothers, we find that one characteristic of their speech to their young children is repetition with variation. This can take a number of forms: A sentence will be offered and then a crucial sub-unit will be extracted and repeated (reduction); a word or phrase will be offered and then included in a larger sentence (expansion); two sentences containing a particular word or phrase in different frames will be offered (variation); two sentences built on a single frame with different items in the slot will be offered (substitution). Here are some examples, taken from a tape made when Minh was 1;2, of consecutive sets of utterances by his mother (the alignments are intended to highlight the repetitive sequences that the child may find useful for

SG:MATCH):[23]

A.
You go *show* mommy.   stress on *show*
   Show mommy.   reduction
   Show mommy whatcha talking about.   expansion/variation

B.
Birdie   birdie.   repetition
Where's birdie?   expansion
   Birdie's we::t.   expansion/lengthening
   Birdie's all *wet* 'cause it's raining.   stress on *wet*

C.
      Chopstick.   theme 1
   That's chopstick.   expansion
      An' you pick up *food* with that.   theme 2
Can you say again chopstick?   expansion of 1
      Chopstick.   repetition/reduction
      Chopstick, to pick up *food*.   reduction/variation
         stress on *food*

(18 turns later)
      Pick up food.   reduction
   Ooh you pick up food like *that*.   expansion

D.
I don't see birdie.
Do you see birdie?   variation
Do you see any doggie too?   substitution

The point here is that such repetitions, expansions, variations, and substitutions in caretaker utterances provide ideal material upon which to apply SG:MATCH and FRAME.

Of course, not all of the speech addressed even to middle-class English-learning children is so ideally suited as this is to the application of segmentation heuristics. And when the input is less than ideal, the child not only will have to work harder to effect plausible segmentations, but may make mistakes in some instances. Evidence for this is found in children's difficulties in dealing with certain chunks of language that are usually encountered as invariant and unsegmented units. Such chunks include (lines of) nursery rhymes, songs, prayers, proverbs, and stereotyped favorite expressions, all of which tend to get presented as nonnegotiable wholes, in the sense that reductions, expansions, and other variations are not considered appropriate or necessary. With this type of input children will have to do the best they can, looking for stresses, lexical items they can identify, morpho-syntactic frames they already know, and so on. It is easy for the researcher to collect

---

[23] Similar sequences have been observed by Snow (1977).

anecdotes about the "cute" misanalyses that result when children try to make sense of such stereotyped language; newspapers and popular magazines regularly contain articles about them. Here are some examples I have collected myself, mostly from friends:[24]

Original	*Misanalysis*
open sesame	open says me
guinea pig	beginning pig
shoo fly	shoe fly
Don Quixote	donkey goat
where the grapes of wrath are stored	where the grapes are wrapped and stored
lead us not into temptation	lead us not into Penn Station
the dawn's early light	the donzerly light
life is but a dream	life is butter and cream
it costs an arm and a leg	it costs a nominal egg
to all intents and purposes	to all intensive purposes
qu'est-ce qui se passe?	qu'est-ce qui space

The same sorts of matching and segmentation strategies seem to have been applied in these instances as in the misperceptions discussed by Browman and by Garnes and Bond, but the lack of variation in these particular frozen phrases, along with their general nonnegotiability, meant that these misanalyses were not subject to correction for a long time, if ever. It is interesting to note that these analyses involve not only lexical matching but the application of grammatical knowledge as well. Thus, in the case of "the donzerly light," the linguist who told me of this (whose name I have forgotten) said that he had no idea what "donzer" meant, but that it had seemed to fit into some sort of adverbial (-*ly*) frame. In a similar vein, when I was a child my grandmother used the expression *scripture measure* whenever anyone overfilled a cup or glass (from *my cup runneth over*). For a long time the best I could do with this was *script your measure* – possibly based on a frame commonly heard by children: Imperative *your* X.[25]

In any case, it is precisely this frozen, formulaic type of language that is least segmentable. This is the epitome of the linguistic "dead end" for the learner, from which it is nearly impossible to extract either lexical or syntactic information. But as we shall see presently, although such language can also be characterized as "routine" in that it is fixed, it does not constitute *all* of input speech that can be so characterized. And *some* "routine" input *can* be extremely helpful for segmentation.

Before we explore "routines" in more depth I first want to consider briefly input speech in one other culture. As we saw in the last chapter, in Trackton,

---

[24] Thanks for some of these examples are due to Elizabeth Barber, John Bisazza, Charles Fillmore, Elizabeth Kimmell, Dennis May, Edward Peters, and Virginia Wayland.

[25] Stephen Boggs suggested this frame to me.

speech to children is not modified along the lines presented at the beginning of this section. That is, it lacks the reductions, expansions, substitutions, and variations intended to enhance the children's comprehension. And yet it is intriguing to discover that, as the Trackton children's linguistic skills develop, children are heard, not only imitating phrases, but also playing with them, manipulating the parts in various ways. Heath calls this stage "repetition with variation" (1983, chap. 3). It seems quite significant that in this community, as in Samoa, such repetition and paraphrase, although not directed to children, are common among adults. In the black community of Trackton it is a valued aspect of a verbal style that is heard in storytelling and prayers (chap. 7); thus repetition with variation may be a strategy that is somehow easily available to children in this community. Heath's description of a language-acquisition process such as the one in Trackton, where children start with long chunks that they then learn to vary on their own, without specially tailored input language from their caretakers but with repetition with variation being modeled in the community, seems particularly important for a theory of segmentation (and language acquisition in general). This is because now we have documentation that children do not need to have language predigested, nor do they have to start at the level of single words in order to acquire language satisfactorily; that is, segmentation heuristics are applicable to a wide range of input. We need to do more studies of input in different cultures with an eye to ways in which it may support or interfere with segmentation processes.

3.4.3. The place of routines in segmentation

In studies of both first- and second-language acquisition the term "routine" has been used in a number of diverse ways. One way, as we have just seen, refers to frozen, nonnegotiable phrases (which we will refer to here as "formulas") from which it is generally difficult to extract either lexical or grammatical information. This is the sense of the term as it is used by Krashen and Scarcella, who refer specifically to memorized phrases such as *How are you?* and *Where is your hotel?* (1978, 283), and by Gleason and Weintraub, who are interested in politeness routines like *thank you* (1978) or in even more situationally specific "routines" such as *trick or treat* (1976).

Other researchers, however, have used the term "routine" in quite a different way, namely, to refer to caretaker–child *interactions* that are predictable in form, both with respect to the content of the individual "lines" (in a dialogue) or "moves" (in a more general interaction) and with respect to their sequencing. Two such routines that have been carefully followed over a period of time for one mother–child pair are the peekaboo game (Ratner & Bruner 1978, for the child Richard between 0;6 and 1;10) and picture-book reading (Ninio & Bruner 1978, for Richard between 0;8 and 1;6). The fixed form of these routines seems to give the child, at quite an early stage, a clear set of expectations upon which to base his participation in the interaction.

But what is of concern to us here is not so much the fixed aspects of the routines as the types of developmental modifications they can undergo. Thus at first – until her child has learned the basic sequence of lines or moves – the mother typically plays both parts, answering or acting for her child, but including him in the action as much as possible. Ratner and Bruner (1978) term this kind of parental support "scaffolding." Thus, in the peekaboo game, the mother at first is the agent who initiates all the moves, hiding either her own face or her son's, removing the mask, and saying "Hello!" on reappearance. Later, when Richard has learned to anticipate the sequence of moves, although she still initiates the game, he joins in more and more on the later moves, helping in the unmasking and beginning to vocalize along with her "Hello!" (398).

And in the book-reading game the mother at first says all the lines, schematized as

1. Look!
2. What's that?
3. It's an X.
4. Yes (an X).   [Ninio & Bruner 1978, 6]

As Richard comes to know the sequence she begins to pause after her question in line 2 in order to allow him to participate by trying to produce the requested label. One effect, then, of such interactive routines is to give the child a predictable way of participating in an interaction. Another effect, at least in the book-reading game (and in its more general form, the labeling game), is to give the child a means of acquiring new labels, both when they are offered by the mother and later when the child learns to ask for them (i.e., to take over lines 1 and 2).

Although the two studies just described have been of interactive routines in which the basic "script" consists of three or four lines or moves, even shorter routines in which each participant has only one line (or move) can develop to support specific communicative needs. Thus, in studying a tape of Minh and his mother made when Minh was 1;2, I found a number of two-line sets that could be classed as routines on the grounds that they occurred more than once, that their form was relatively fixed, and that each such set had an identifiable communicative function. One such routine was used by Minh to get a response from his mother:

  Minh: Mommy!
Mother: What? / Huh? / Yes?

Another was used to call attention to a particular object:

Minh: Ooh! (breathy voice)
Mother: What? (or some other response directed toward the object Minh was focused on)

Still a third routine was used to signal that something had dropped:

Minh: Oh-oh!
Mother: What did you do? / Pick 'em up.

It is significant that even at so young an age as 14 months, when his non-routine language was neither particularly well developed nor very intelligible, Minh was able to use these little routines quite effectively as communication supports. The fact that he had learned these routines from others, much in the manner described by Bruner and his associates, is also evident on this tape, since his mother also initiates both the *Ooh* and *Oh-oh* routines, whereas Minh's older brother clearly uses (and thus models) the *Mommy* routine several times. Thus the communicative support that Minh is able to draw on here is tied to the fact that his interactants know the routines too, and can use the predictable formats to figure out Minh's communicative intent when he invokes a given routine. Looking for such routines, then, may offer us an important insight into how children get hold of communicatively useful chunks of language so as to be able to participate in rudimentary conversations very early, much as Wong Fillmore's second-language learners did.

But this is not all there is to be said about such interactive routines. Although they may be fixed at first, both in the sequence of communicative moves and in the content of each line, there is evidence that they may go on to develop in interesting ways. As we have just seen, one of the first developments concerns which participant makes each move in the still-fixed sequence. Thus at first the mother makes all the moves, but indicates to her child which moves might be construed to be his. As he comes to know the sequence so that he can anticipate certain key moves, she encourages him to participate, leaving pauses for him to make a try, taking his turn if he does not, reinforcing him if he does. As he comes to participate more reliably she acts as a "communication ratchet" (Bruner 1978, 254) by insisting on his participation where she knows he can do it, while supporting and encouraging participation in more marginal situations.

As with the formulaic chunks of language discussed earlier, if variation is present we would expect segmentation to occur, but if the situation does not allow for variation we would expect stagnation. Ratner and Bruner (1978) observed that the peekaboo game went through a developmental sequence until Richard could play both parts, but then died out as he lost interest. The book-reading situation, however, allows for more variation. Once a child has learned to produce labels in the proper slot (line 3), and then to request labels her- or himself (by playing the other part, using lines 1 and 2), new kinds of moves can be added, for example, requesting the noise a pictured animal is alleged to make, labeling parts of pictures, relating pictures to personal experiences, and so on. Thus a more open-ended routine potentially provides support for several kinds of linguistic and communicative development. How much of this potentiality will actually be taken advantage of may depend on cultural factors: Heath (1983, chap. 7) describes how in a community that she calls Roadville even book reading reaches a dead end quite early.

Snow (1981b) describes the book-reading routine at a later stage, as it had developed between herself and her son Nathaniel by the time he was 2½ years old. Her data are taken from eight tapes in which they were looking at the same book from one session to the next. She shows how, within the by then well-known format of the routine, N is able to make progressive use of information he receives from his mother. Thus at one session a new topic (and label) may be jointly introduced (these examples are taken from Snow's Table 7):

N: Who's that?
M: X.
N: X.
M: X, right.

At a subsequent session N may reintroduce the topic, using the recently acquired label, which his mother confirms before she offers more information about this topic:

N: Who's that X.
M: X, right. What's X doing?
N: X doing?
M: X is Y-ing.
N: X Y-ing.

The expression and development of topic X may get carried yet a step further in a still later session, with N again introducing the topic at the level of his expanded ability:

N: X Y-ing.
M: That's right.
N: X have?
M: X has a Z.
N: a Z.
M: Right, a Z.

Again we see that interactive routines that allow for variation and expansion are neither linguistic nor communicative dead ends, but rather offer an important kind of support for growth in which the learner may even have some control over how fast new information is offered.

As we can see, in order for researchers to pursue the implications of these observations it is necessary both to broaden and to restrict the notion of "routine." We must broaden it in the sense that the criterion for recognition can no longer be that its form is absolutely fixed, for it is precisely its possibilities for variation that engender linguistic development. Thus the "sameness" can only be relative – within a fixed general framework that is allowed (expected) to develop over time. The general communicative function of a particular routine, however, might be expected to remain more constant. Another important point is that these routines must be studied over time so as to reveal how changes in their format contribute to the child's developing linguistic and communicative systems.

On the other hand, our ideas of routines must be more focused in that we must expect to discover routines that serve specific functions, and we must expect that routines which serve different functions will contribute in different ways to the child's linguistic knowledge. We have seen how the book-reading routine contributes to the segmentation and learning of various kinds of labels. Several recent studies have looked at ways in which parental requests for narratives of personal experience (e.g., "Tell Daddy what we did today") can provide support for learning not only culturally accepted norms for structuring stories (appropriate sequencing of appropriate topics) but also correct linguistic forms for doing so (Eisenberg 1981; Sachs 1977b; Stoel-Gammon & Cabral 1977; see also discussion in Cazden 1979). In a similar vein, Johnson (1980) shows how children can acquire such specific linguistic material as question words by starting with "set phrases tied to very specific interaction routines" (1), which the children only slowly segment into appropriate constituents. We need to follow up on these pioneering studies by selecting specific linguistic structures and possible associated communicative functions, and then looking for routines that might serve to support the acquisition of these structures and functions. These routines must then be recorded and described, with attention paid not only to changes in the type of support available but also to the strategies children use to discover the linguistic information available to them in these routines.

3.4.4. *Individual differences*

In 2.2.4 I discussed individual differences among children with respect to the extraction process. A few more remarks are in order as I conclude this look at segmentation and perception of structural patterns, if only to raise questions for further research.

If a child makes heavy productive use of frames of the constant + variable type, the aggregate of her or his productions will have what has been termed the "pivot look."[26] It has recently been noted by several researchers that this pivot look may be more characteristic of some children than others (Bloom, Lightbown, & Hood 1975; Horgan 1980; Nelson 1981). In fact Horgan (1980, 7–8) and Nelson (1981, 173) suggest that Expressive/Noun-leaver children may tend to rely on patterns of the constant + variable type, whereas Referential/Noun-lover children may be more likely to produce variable + variable constructions.

The sequencing of analysis and production may be crucial in the creation of a pivot look. Accordingly, if a child is productively cautious and does a great deal of analysis before saying much, the child's sentence frames may quickly become of the variable + variable (nonpivot) type. However, a child who is eager to talk may not wait upon her or his analysis but rely heavily on "formulas"(useful extracted units) and "pivot constructions" (constant + variable frames). Like Wong Fillmore's Nora (1976), such a child may produce freely, relying on feedback to guide evaluation of her or his productions.

More work is needed to sort out these differences among children in segmentation and pattern perception strategies. For instance, how much of these differences might be due to innate preferences for processing language in certain ways (e.g., "pattern extractors" vs. "builder uppers"), as opposed to differences in the uses to which language is to be put, input variables, and/or cultural factors?

---

[26] The term "pivot" refers to Braine's (1963) suggestion that children's two-word combinations could be described in terms of two classes of words: "pivots," which constitute a closed class of words that occur with high frequency in fixed positions (corresponding to the "constant" terms in our frames), and an "X" (or "open") class of words that can combine with the pivots or with each other (the "variable" terms). Although "pivot grammars" as such have been abandoned as a useful description of the two-word stage, the "pivot look" is still recognized as a real phenomenon that has to be dealt with in some other way (Brown 1973). Moreover, Braine's work on "limited scope formulae," already discussed in 3.2, can be seen as a revision and extension of his ideas on pivot grammars.

4   The role of units in production

We have just spent two chapters looking at ways in which linguistic units are acquired through extraction and segmentation, and ways in which knowledge of these units and their structural patterns can be used in the comprehension of language. It is not necessary, however, for a unit to be fully segmented (in adult terms), or, indeed, segmented at all, before it can be put to use in the production of new utterances. In fact, treating an unanalyzed or only partially analyzed chunk of language as if it were unitary would allow learners to produce utterances that seem otherwise to be beyond their productive competence.

Although many early productions are easily seen as combinations of two or more adult words, there is a heretofore confusing residue of data that are not so readily seen in this light. If, however, we agree that children may have units in a variety of sizes, from a variety of sources, as well as a variety of ways of combining them, we will find it easier to make sense of these data.

One purpose of this chapter, therefore, is to review some of the data on early productions (some of which we have already looked at in the context of perception and analysis) from the point of view of the combination of long as well as short units. I will proceed by considering a number of strategies children seem to use in producing multi-unit constructions and by seeing the roles played by long units. I will be particularly interested in how the use of long units can make up for both the shortage of cognitive capacity and the incomplete analysis of the language.

Having established that long units may effectively persist well beyond the early stages of language perception, I will move on to the second aim of this chapter, which is to consider the role of long units in adult language. I am interested in such questions as: What happens to a "long unit" (i.e., one that contains two or more morphemes of the adult language) after it has been segmented? Is the fact that it was once perceived as unitary completely lost? Or might at least some of these long units maintain a dual status as units and as analyzed sequences of smaller units? Are new long units ever created (fused) out of smaller units? What might be the role of processing limitations and automatization of patterns of language use in the creation and maintenance of long units? I will defer a discussion of the theoretical consequences of the coexistence of long and short units until the next chapter.

4.1. Children's multi-unit productions

4.1.1. *Production strategies using two units*

As children develop both cognitively and in gaining control of those units of the language they have isolated, they begin to produce two-unit utterances, that is, to "synthesize" speech. For some children this transition from one unit to two may be very slow and easy to follow (once the observer realizes what is happening). This transparency is increased if the units the child is working with are primarily single adult words. This was the case, for instance, with Brenda, the child studied by Scollon, who went through several discernible stages as she progressed from successive but related one-word utterances, each with its own intonation contour (Scollon's "vertical constructions"), to more fluently produced constructions with a single primary stress and a single intonation contour (Scollon's "horizontal constructions," 1976, chap. 7).

For other children, however, the transition from one unit to two may take place less obviously, and/or the units involved may be relatively long, so that the process is much more difficult for the linguist to trace: When long constituents are prevalent, the linguist constantly has to be making judgments about which parts have been constructed by the child and which parts might be formulaic units (see the discussion in 1.3.1). The possibility that a child might be using long units also forces the researcher to consider whether the child's competence is what it appears to be on the surface or whether it is less. Further difficulties arise when a tendency to produce long sentencelike utterances is coupled with garbled phonology, as it was with Minh. In such a case, the transition to two units is virtually impossible to document.

Pseudosynthesis using a "carrier."   I felt that Minh sometimes tried to sound as though he were producing sentences, without really synthesizing at all; that is, he was embedding a single information-bearing unit in a lot of sentencelike "carriers." For example:

In some of Minh's early Tunes [i.e., phrases approximated by their intonational melodies], in addition to the fairly well-analysed parts, there were "filler syllables" which seemed to be used as place-holders to fill out not yet analysed parts of a phrase. Thus, between 14 and 15 months, when something fell on the floor, Minh would exclaim: ⟨'ó'o, dʌdʌdʌ⟩ 'uh-oh, x x x'.

. . . The fixed [part, ⟨'ó'o⟩, was] reproduced faithfully; but the variable [part] seemed to be less well analysed, and [was] represented by place-holders like ⟨dʌdʌ⟩ and ⟨dʌdʌ dʌ⟩. [Peters 1977, 564]

From anecdotes that have been reported to me, I suspect that quite a few children use this strategy, although it has not yet been systematically documented.

Synthesis by juxtaposing two units.   Sometimes children seem to be combining two longish units, although more typically there is one long unit and one short unit. Some of the best examples of synthesis with long units come from Clark, who describes a number of phenomena that seem to reflect the fact that children are working with long units. One of these she calls Imitation; another she calls Coupling. She notes that "representations of adult utterances may be stored by children in the form in which they perceive them, without being reproduced immediately. These are imitations in the sense that they owe their form to the fact that they are copied from an adult model, rather than being constructed by the child from elements" (1977, 341). She goes on to observe:

There are two possibilities that have been overlooked in claims that many utterances by children deviate too much from adult utterances to be regarded as faithful or reduced imitations. Firstly, a child's utterance may originate as a copy of a part of an adult utterance; it may be an EXTRACT of an adult utterance. Secondly, a portion of a child's utterance may originate as an imitation, even when the whole utterance does not; this imitated portion may be combined or COUPLED with other material to produce a longer utterance which does deviate from its adult equivalent by more than the omission of elements. [342–3]

Later she remarks, "Many mistakes in the speech of my own two sons can be readily explained in terms of the imitation of elliptical utterances which are then coupled with other constituents to produce a longer utterance . . . The combination entails no internal modification of the parts" (344). That is, Imitations are unanalyzed units, and Coupling is the juxtaposition of such units to produce longer utterances. Thus the children seem to have been forming two-unit constructions exactly as expected at this stage, but the units were not single adult words.

Clark illustrates this process with her son Ivan's early use of possessive pronouns:

The sequence *That's mine* originated as an immediate imitation. He used this for some time, then at about two years of age he began to couple this sequence with noun phrases e.g. *That's mine jam* 2;0.11. To begin with, these combinations had the prosodic characteristics of two successive utterances . . . but gradually he came to produce them with one contour . . . Whilst *That's mine jam* does not appear to be the product of imitation (since it could not be modelled directly on an adult utterance), it seems quite clear that it came about through the imitation of a short sentence, which was then rehearsed frequently, and finally combined with another constituent. Only gradually did the parts become fused within one intonation contour. Once a sequence is established it may be difficult for the child to modify it. He simply incorporates it as it stands into his longer utterances. [344]

It is striking that in this example Ivan's construction *That's mine* + *jam* seems to start out as a vertical construction (in Scollon's terms – i.e., with two intonation contours) and only gradually becomes a horizontal construction (with a single contour). That is, the process entirely parallels Brenda's early two-word constructions, with only the size of the units being different.

Clark's Coupling is similar to what Moerk and Moerk (1979) refer to as Quotations (copied from nursery books, songs, or nursery rhymes) and Imitations (copied from speech), and what Snow (1981a) calls Expanded Imitations. The following example from Snow shows imitations of portions of adult utterances being combined with the recently acquired *No:*

(10)   M: Oh, king Nathaniel. (wrapping N up in towel)
       N: No king Nathaniel.
       M: Is   Nathaniel a king?
       N: No Nathaniel a king.
       M: What's Nathaniel?
       N: No king Nathaniel.   [210, alignment mine]

Another of Clark's examples of Coupling involves the juxtaposition of questions and answers:

For a period [Ivan] would repeat adult questions rather than answering them. Later he began to answer questions after repeating them, and finally, he would ask the questions himself and provide his own answers, e.g. *Where's Adam? Upstairs* (2;1.17). Having produced the successive utterances, he would then often integrate them in one intonation contour: *Where's Adam upstairs?* [1977, 354]

Questions and answers, of course, regularly occur next to each other in the input (see the discussion of the *What's that?* routine in 3.4.3), so perhaps it is not surprising that a child should incorporate them into a single utterance.

Minh, too, went through a short period of asking a question and then answering it, sometimes including the two within a single intonation contour. There is an example of this in my data at 1;8.20, when he seemed particularly to be working on the question–answer sequence *What's that? That's* X. He had already been using the form [sæ] or [ʌsæ] for a long time to mean 'What's that?' On this day, however, he used the same phonological form (⟨sæ⟩) to mean both 'What's that?' and 'that's' – something he had not done before. (Earlier he had used forms such as [ŋ] or [hɪ] with a deictic function.) The fact that on this day he was working on the question–answer sequence was suggested to me by his mother, who, referring to my usual practice of spending some time looking at a book with Minh, said, "The ideal situation of course is for him to

read it by himself – because he does *your* part an' *his* part at the same [time]."
And indeed, he did tend to use ⟨sæ⟩ both for asking for words he didn't know
(seven times) and for pointing out words he did know (thirty-nine times). An
example of the use of ⟨sæ⟩ to ask for a word he did not know is

AP: What's that?
 M: [sæ]?
AP: Fly.
 M: fay.

In pointing out words he did know, Minh seemed to be making use of a
frame with a single slot: ⟨sæ⟩ + N. Whether this was derived from question
+ answer *(What's that?* X) or from statement + continuation *(That's* X) is hard
to tell. A third possibility is that *What's that* and *That's* were as yet phonologically indistinguishable to him and thus perceived as interchangeable.
Whatever its source, of the instances of ⟨sæ⟩ + N, twenty-five occurred with
them both included in the same intonation contour, whereas fourteen were
not so incorporated. In one instance the degree of integration seemed to
change from one utterance to the next:

AP: Here's a –
 M: [sæ? bʊdi] (nearly one contour) 'What's that? Birdie'.
AP: Little birdie.
 M: [sæ budɪh] (one contour) 'That's a birdie'.

In any case, Minh seems to have been treating ⟨sæ⟩, which by any analysis
consists of more than one unit in an adult system, as if it were no different
structurally from *birdie* or *fly:* It could be used in synthesis before it was broken
down into its adult constituents.

Clark found it necessary to invent the terms "Coupling," "Imitation," and
"Extract" in order to describe situations in which a child uses unanalyzed
stretches of speech that are no longer than single adult words. From the child's
point of view, however, these phenomena are no different from the juxtaposition
of any other units to produce longer utterances.

4.1.2. *Production strategies using more than two units*

The child's ability to handle language grows in terms of the number of
acquired units and length of the constructions that can be synthesized, as well
as in terms of grammatical complexity. The strategy of using ready-made
wholes, which are either stored as such in the lexicon or extracted from
recently heard speech, as a basis for synthesis may nevertheless persist long
after the two-unit stage. Just as at the two-unit stage, such a strategy would
allow children to make the most of what they know even while their ability to

handle complex constructions is still rather limited. At this later stage, however, it is increasingly likely that these ready-made wholes are not completely unanalyzed, but that at least some lexico-semantic extraction and recognition has occurred even if the syntactic details are not yet under full control. In fact, it is the existence of minor syntactic anomalies that gives the researcher clues about the presence of incompletely analyzed chunks. Let us look at the evidence, this time proceeding from more sophisticated to less sophisticated strategies.

Juxtaposing two constructions.   In the following examples from Clark's son, Ivan, although he has clearly progressed past the two-unit stage it is not clear exactly how many units there are in each utterance. Clark remarks that they each seem to be "AMALGAMS of two different utterances" (1977, 345):

That's not the right thing   I wanted to do.   (3;8.22)
Why didn't you   allowed to shut the door?   (4;5.9)

The spacing I have imposed here is meant to suggest a segmentation into plausible familiar phrases from which Ivan probably constructed these utterances. Although in each case there is a syntactic anomaly where the familiar phrases join, these utterances are both rather sophisticated. Similar examples of this same strategy can be seen in the following, this time from Adam Clark:

(16) Let me down, *ride my bike.*
(17) I don't know *where's Emma gone.*   [Clark 1974, 6]

Putting a construction in a frame.   Some of Adam Clark's utterances seem to have been based on formulaic frames that had slots that could contain whole sentences, for example, *I want* + S, *Where's* + S:

(14) I want   *you get a biscuit for me.*
(20) I want   *I eat apple.*
(19) Where's *the boy brought the milk.*   (Looking for the milk the boy had brought)
        [Clark 1974, 5–6, alignment mine]

In a similar manner Kelly Horgan at 2;0 constructed requests for actions by using the frame *How about* + S:

How about daddy go get a hamburger?
How about open more presents?   (said the day after Christmas)
How about what do you want to eat?   (meaning 'Ask me what I want to eat')
        [Horgan 1980, 19, alignment mine]

In these examples the communicative goal is achieved through reliance on known units and formulaic frames well before full syntactic analysis has been accomplished.

Building on a previous (adult) utterance (part of) which is taken as unitary. Another way to take maximal advantage of preexisting units is to build on (a part of) an adult's previous utterance. Ivan Clark used this strategy, which Clark calls Incorporation, in the following examples:[27]

Mother: We're all very mucky.
  Child: I   all very mucky too.
Mother: Do you want to get off?
  Child: No I   want to get on.
Mother: That's   upside down.
  Child: No, I want to upside down.   [1974, 3, alignments mine]

   In Iwamura's study of the two 3-year-olds Nani and Suzy (1979, 1980), we find that one day Nani constructed a sentence in which she seems to have synthesized a (perhaps formulaic) phrase, "I don' wanna," with Suzy's previous sentence, "Don't throw":

1 S: Don't throw. Don't throw.
2 N: I don' wanna don' throw.   [1979, 3]

A child can even use such a strategy to construct *yes/no* questions from their major surface constituents without having to learn how to invert subject and auxiliary. As Clark describes it:

Yes/no questions entered Adam's speech at 3;2 when he began to extract question tags from the end of adult utterances. After a few days of regularly copying tags, he began the practice of copying them and then coupling them with other elements, e.g. Adult: *It's cold, isn't it?* Adam: *Isn't it? Isn't it dark, too?* Up to this time the only sequence resembling a *yes/no* question in Adam's repertoire had been *shall we.* This appeared to be an unanalysed routine, with no internal structure, since he did not use *we* in any other context, and the phrase subsequently dropped out of his speech. [1977, 344]

This is reminiscent of the simple question-construction tactics described in the previous section.

Building on one's own construction. Another tactic for producing utterances whose complexity is just a bit beyond one's productive capacity is to work up to the goal in stages. Clark notes that her son Adam did this; she calls it Buildup, since he would build upon his own previous utterances: "There was a tendency for the whole of the previous utterance to be retained as a constituent of, or framework for, the subsequent utterance" (1974, 2). For example:

        Baby Ivan have a bath,
let's go see *baby Ivan have a bath*.   [2, alignment mine]

---

[27] Note that we have already seen the first two of these examples in 3.1.2. There, however, our focus was on the perception of units, whereas here we are interested in the uses to which extracted units can be put.

This same approach is found in Iwamura, where Nani (2;9) is trying to get an answer to her question and varies only the beginning:

Are   you   come to *our* house, Suzy?
Do   you   come to *our* house?
Does Suzy come to *our* house, Mommy?
Is   Suzy come to *our* house?   [1980, 61]

In another example from Iwamura, as Nani (3;6) struggles with the pronoun *she/her*, she retains the rest of the structure of the sentence until the very end:

I don' wan' she
I don' wan' she   to talk to me.
I don' wan' him, she to talk to me.
  Don' wan' Suzy   to talk to me.
I don' wan' you   to talk to me.
  Don' wan'
  Don'   talk to me.   [88]

Several strategies at once.   Sometimes the linguist is lucky and not only is privileged to hear the fission happen before her or his very ears, but is able to isolate what must have been the clue that allowed it to happen. This is the case with the following complex example (from Clark), which involves incorporation from another's utterance as well as building on the child's own utterance. Clark describes this as an instance of what she calls "the accidental juxtaposition of alternative forms":

At 2;11 Ivan said, watching me run water into the bath *You want to have a bath?* This seems to have originated as an extract from *Do you want to have a bath?* He then picked up his teddy and produced, apparently through coupling, the sentence *I want teddy have a bath*. A few moments later he modified this to *I want teddy to have a bath*, apparently under the influence of the extract which he had used a minute or two earlier. [1977, 356]

Thus, because of the closeness in time of the two sentences *You want to have a bath?* and *I want teddy have a bath,* Ivan was able to figure out that *to* should be inserted in the latter sentence to produce a more adultlike form. Presumably his first try (*I want teddy have a bath*) was constructed on the pattern I want + S (which there is evidence – given earlier in this section – that he used). Perhaps the existence of this earlier pattern allowed him to segment his mother's utterance as *Do you want + to have a bath* rather than *Do you want to + have a bath,* or else he might have said *I want to teddy have a bath.* [28]

This quick tour of a number of children's early productions should serve to show how, through use of strategies such as extraction (Imitation) and juxtaposition (Coupling), and with the aid of such elementary syntactic patterns as formulaic frames with single analyzed slots, the child who is capable of only rudimentary synthesis may be able to produce quite sophisticated-sounding utter-

---

[28] This was pointed out to me by Susan Fischer.

ances. It is an important challenge to the linguist confronted with such data to determine just how far the child's grammatical knowledge actually extends.

The nonunitary nature of units. In most of the preceding examples the long units involved seem to have undergone some segmentation and assignment of meaning, but they were certainly not completely analyzed with respect to their structural details. In the interests of achieving a desired communicative goal it may have been easier to concentrate on the overall appropriateness and to forget about the details. Pronoun shifting seems to be a particularly difficult detail to work out: Phrases containing pronouns are often used just as they were heard by a child; consider, for instance, the *I carry you* and *sit my knee* examples quoted in 1.3.1. Snow has a number of examples of this, including:

(11) M: I'm going to throw Nathaniel away. One two three whoosh.
        Throw you away.
    N: /ɛnə/ throw you away   again.   (/ɛnə/ = 'wanna')

(12) M: Ya gonna get me?
    N: /ɛnə/   get me   again.   [1981a, 210, alignments mine]

Age 2;9. Coming downstairs before breakfast, wearing pyjamas with fabric feet in them, N said at the top of the stairs "The pj's you got on are slippery." There had been no mention to him of pj's on that day. His mother had said to him "The pj's you've got on are slippery" as he was walking down the stairs the previous morning. [1981b, 25]

Age 2;9. As he started to climb up on low walls or other objects which required balance to walk on, N would typically say "Let's see you climb up on this one." This was the utterance frequently used by his father in encouraging him to walk on such structures. [1981b, 25]

A gradual transition from unanalyzed to partly analyzed to fully analyzed forms is also supported by Moerk and Moerk's observation that "utterances that were at first obviously imitated after a parental model are reemployed by the child and are slowly incorporated into his spontaneous repertoire. During this beginning mastery period parental models can still serve as 'reinstatements', 'memory help,' or 'releasers', so that the transition is fully continuous." (1979, 47).

Many of the examples that we have been looking at seem to support the notion that partially analyzed chunks of speech can be used in productions as if they were unitary. Might it also be true that, for speed of processing, even fully analyzed units can still be used as if they were unitary? If this is true, then such constructions must be producible in more than one way: as unitary items (retrieved whole from memory) and as constructions (produced by the grammar). I will explore the theoretical implications of this possibility in the next chapter. A further implication, which will concern us here, is that novel constructions may actually be created, and be stored away and retrieved as units in spite of their known nonunitary status.

4.2. Fusion: the creation of new units

Just as linguistic chunks that were originally acquired as wholes can slowly be segmented into smaller constituents, so, too, it seems that language users often build up convenient constructions that they file away as units for future use. Sometimes these constructions eventually acquire such specialized usages that the original meanings are no longer recoverable from their surface structures, in which case they achieve the status of idioms. This can happen among a small group of contemporary speakers, as well as across several generations of speakers. In any case, it seems that the original impetus to store away such prefabricated sequences is to achieve maximal expressive effectiveness with minimal processing. I will take a little space to explore how such shortcuts seem to work for adults, both synchronically and diachronically, before looking at evidence for them in language acquisition.

4.2.1. *Fused constructions for adults*

Considered from a purely practical point of view, if a speaker has found, through trial and error, an expression that seems to convey a particular idea especially effectively, she or he has a strong motivation to remember that construction. Then the next time the speaker is discussing the topic to which the expression is relevant, she or he can use it whole, shortcutting the constructive stage and saving energy for some other aspect of the discourse. Thus Bateson observes that

> virtually all speech is studded with preformed sequences, sometimes only a couple of words long and sometimes full paragraphs long, which, although internally ordered by syntactic rules that would allow their novel generation, are used as single building blocks and are inserted as single items. I do not use written lectures in my teaching, and the selection and organization of topics is different every year, but floating in the stream of new combinations are great lumps that have been used before, some of them many times, which are generally not recognizable as replays to the student who hears them for the first time, because they are governed by the same linguistic code. [1975, 61]

Probably anyone who has tried to express a given idea more than once, whether it be in a classroom lecture, a shaggy dog story, or the recounting of an exciting incident, has (unconsciously) used the strategy of memorizing the parts that went over well in order to have them available the next time. Many people even resort to rehearsal, trying out different wordings in the absence of any audience until a particularly apt one is found and then practicing it until it is smooth enough for quick retrieval.

One of the reasons that fused speech is so difficult to talk about is that it is not an all-or-none affair and there are at least two relatively independent continua involved: one a scale of grammatical transparency/opacity, the other having to do with the size of community for which a particular expression has become fused. Such a community can range from a single person who has memorized especially apt expressions for later retrieval, through intimate societies of two and other small closed groups, on up to large speech communities, for example, all speakers of English who watch certain television shows. On the transparency/opacity scale fused speech can range from the grammatically transparent "lumps" that Bateson called attention to; through collocations such as *I'm so glad you could bring Harry*, which, although formed according to the rules of English grammar, do have certain restrictions on their usage (e.g., Pawley & Syder point out that it is unnatural, although in fact perfectly grammatical, to say *That you could bring Harry makes me so glad* [1976, 33]); to idioms such as *kick the bucket* for which the meaning is not recoverable through grammatical analysis. Such expressions correspond to Hayes-Roth's notion of "assemblies" that can become "strengthened" to the point of "unitization" (1977, 261).

When one carefully considers how these two continua might interrelate, it seems clear that those expressions which an individual has unilaterally stored for her or his own use (which I called "idiosyncratic formulas" in 1.1) must of necessity be grammatically transparent, since they must be analyzable by the hearers. These "formulas" are therefore indistinguishable from newly generated speech (except perhaps on the basis of fluency; see Pawley & Syder 1976). On the other hand, as soon as meaning can be negotiated, as in a linguistic community of two or more, violations of grammar (e.g., ellipsis) can also be negotiated, a process that gives rise to the more syntactically opaque expressions characteristic of intimate speech (Joos 1967), jargon, ritual (Bateson 1975), technical language, and all other kinds of ingroup speech. In fact, the very opacity of certain expressions can be used as a sort of verbal fence to include certain hearers who have the knowledge to decode the expressions and to exclude those others who lack that knowledge.

Turning now to diachronic evidence, some of the phenomena I would classify as fusion have been described by other linguists as the formation, through such processes as derivation and compounding, of new wordlike expressions that are then lexicalized. Bolinger (1975, chap. 5) gives many examples of English words that have recently been fused by such processes. This same drive for efficiency is also evident in sign language, as is apparent in Frishberg's illustrations of the development of compounds in American Sign Language over a period of 100 to 200 years. For example, although the current sign for HOME originally evolved from a transparent combination of the two signs EAT and SLEEP, in contemporary conversational signing this origin is no longer apparent, since the two parts have assimilated to each other in both handshape and location. Frishberg notes that "the tendency for signs to become single units, i.e. not to remain compounds, is very strong" (1975, 710). She also points out that this tendency toward unitization of compounds benefits not only the signer, since "maximizing fluid movement minimizes the signer's articulation difficulties" (710–11), but also the viewer, "by clearly marking the beginning and end of a given lexical item, indicating that it is indeed a single item" (711).

An extreme form of lexicalization of fused forms can be found in the creation (aided by phonological assimilation and reduction) of portmanteau morphemes such as French *de le > du, de les > des,* or German *zu dem > zum, von dem > vom.*

4.2.2. *Fused constructions for children*

Turning now to the place of fusion in language learning, evidence can be found that children also fuse speech sequences, seemingly as shortcuts to avoid having to construct them anew each time. This strategy, of course, makes perfect sense in view of the evidence that small children are, more than anyone, handicapped by short-term processing limitations, and the belief that they would be glad to take advantage of any available means, including memorization, to help overcome these limitations. Thus we find children adopting stereotyped expressions that are neither copied directly from nor even directly reduced from adult usage, giving evidence that some sort of construction process may have gone on before the expression became frozen.

Before looking at evidence for children's fusions, let us first note that MacWhinney also proposes that combinations generated by the child are stored in the lexicon. In his model of the acquisition of morphophonology he suggests that "once the child is able to produce forms by combination, he is able to pick up forms that he himself has created . . . All combinations that do not lead to disequilibrated pairs [i.e., discrepancies within the child's own system] are placed in file 1 [the child's file of words]" (1978, 12).

An example of a child's fusion can be seen in Minh's expression ⟨kamun⟩ (3.3). The constituents were originally extracted from the beginning and the end of "the cow jumping over the moon," but they were subsequently fused with each other and then with the word *Daddy* to form "cow moon Daddy." As I interpret my data, it was through repetition of this last fused phrase that the element ⟨ka⟩ lost its reference to "cow" and acquired its demonstrative/existential character. Another expression that Minh adapted for his own usage, possibly through phonological misanalysis and metathesis, but more probably through combination of ⟨kamun⟩ with yet another word, is the title of the book *Good Night Moon*, which he referred to as "Cow Moon Night" (⟨kamʊn⟩ night) for at least two months (1;7.2 to 1;8.27).

Similarly, Weir discusses two "original compounds" formed by her son Anthony, age 2½: "One, *bathing room*, is used in addition to the standard *bathroom*. The new-formation was probably coined by analogy with 'bathing suit,' a word well known to the child. The other neologism is *phone call book*, a coinage due to the child's greater familiarity with *phone call* than merely 'phone'" (1962, 75).

In Iwamura's data (1980) we find some nice examples of how these two 3-year-olds, in their back-seat society of two, were capable of evolving fused phrases that had meaning only for their particular dyad (and, of course, for the linguist who eavesdropped on the process). A simple example is Nani and Suzy's transformation of a disagreement into the neologism [nowɪs]. On May 13 Suzy (3;8) tried to tell Nani (3;5) what to do, but Nani successfully managed to turn the interchange into what Iwamura calls an Antonym Game, with Suzy saying "No" and Nani saying "Yes" (four times each). Since Suzy was still trying to influence Nani's behavior, Nani then tried a new tactic; she told Suzy, "I say no and you say no," and again, "You say yes and I say no" (209). Not only was this the first instance of what Iwamura calls the You Say Game, but it also laid the foundation for a follow-up incident a week later (May 20). This time an adult question ("Have a nice day, girls?") produced a chorused "Ye-e-s," after which Nani started to repeat "No–yes" (five times). She then, using the "You say X" format introduced the previous week, instructed Suzy "You say no–yes, no–yes." The idea caught on, and the girls took turns repeating "no–yes" and instructing the other girl to say it:

1.   D: Have a nice day, girls?

2.   S&N: (unison) Ye-e-s.

3.   N: (giggle) No–yes, no–yes, no–yes, no–yes, no–yes. You say no–yes, no–yes.

4.   S: Say no–yes, no–yes.

5.   N: No–yes, no–yes, no–yes, no–yes. Say no–yes, no–yes.
     (short pause)

6.   N: You say [nowɪs]. You say, no–yes.

7.   S: {You say / I 'ready say no–yes

8.   N: No you didn', I didn' *hear*.

9.   S: You say [nowɪs nowɪs].

10. N: No, you say no–yes.

11. S: I *did*.

12. N: I didn't *hear* you.

13.   S: (faster, more slurred) [nowɪs nowɪs nowɪs nowɪs]. Your turn say
        [nowɪsnowɪs].
etc.   [120–1]

We can see here exactly how the fusion of "no–yes" to [nowɪs] took place: It was introduced in line 6, but Nani also repeated the full form immediately after, as if to make clear what she meant. Then Suzy picked up the fused form in line 9. Finally, from line 13 on, the fused form seems to have been accepted by both girls.

Iwamura gives another interesting example of the evolution of a fused lexical item in the case of "down-floor-dress." One day when Suzy was 3;9 and Nani was 3;6 they had a long discussion concerning long dresses (muumuus), covering the fact that they were each wearing "a long dress down to the floor" and a clarification of what "down to the floor" meant: " 'Down to the floor' had at least three meanings on 12 June: (1) covering the legs, going toward the floor . . . ; (2) touching the floor . . . ; and (3) falling down or off" (209). Two days later (June 14) when the topic of long dresses came up again, the girls evolved their own "word" (i.e., fused expression) for the concept:

1. N: Is it a long dress?
2. S: Yes.
3. N: I'm wearing a long dress.
4. S: I ⌠too.
5. N: ⌊Is that one is a down-to-the-floor dress?
6. S: Uh-huh.
7. N: Is it a down-floor dress?
8. S: Uh-huh, mines down.   [90]

In order to show the development of the phrase Iwamura diagrams the questions (1,5,7) as follows:

1. N: Is it	a long	dress?
5. N: Is that one is	a down-to-the-floor	dress?
7. N: Is it	a down-floor	dress? [90]

She comments:

In 7, [Nani] reduced "that one" to "it" and "down-to-the-floor" to "down-floor." Thus, the last question in the series was exactly like the first except that "long" was expressed as "down-floor." Nani lexicalized a syntactic unit by removing the functor words *to* and *the*, thus eliminating the surface prepositional phrase, and ended up with a single lexical unit. *Down-floor* was pronounced as a unit (like *pants-suit* or *after-dinner drink*) and was interchangeable with "long" . . . [This example] provides enough history of *down-floor* as a lexical unit to suggest that such shortened forms in children's speech are not always the result of their inability to deal with complex forms . . . The *down-floor* example suggests that a step which can follow the analysis of a whole into its parts may be the deletion of appropriate (i.e., deletable) parts. [91]

Such neologisms by children give tantalizing evidence of the fusion process, and yet to my knowledge they have never been systematically looked at to see what light they can shed on children's need for shortcutting devices and the way they make use of a combination of constructive ability and memorization to achieve the needed relief. (The study of such shortcuts can, however, be confounded by the fact that the creations are often so charming that they are adopted and perpetuated by the family as part of its intimate speech code.)

4.3. Lexical redundancy and automatization of patterns

We spent Chapter 3 looking at how language learners break extracted units down into their constituent sub-units and structural patterns. In this chapter we have been looking at ways in which children and adults make use of or even create long units. If units can be both broken down (fissioned) and created (fused), what is the theoretical status of the notion "lexical unit" from the point of view of linguistic performance? That is, is there, as current linguistic theory would have us believe, a single clearly identifiable level of analysis that can be designated as basic for the language user? Or might there be more than one such level? Before we commit ourselves to a position with regard to this question, let us first consider in what ways multiple levels of units could be useful to language users.

What sorts of situations might lead language users to want to be able to store and retrieve chunks of language in more than one way? I will suggest three: Two involve partial but incomplete analysis of chunks by language learners, whereas the third leads to processing efficiency for mature language users.

1. A language learner may have learned a useful chunk of language and may be able to do some identification of sub-units without yet being able to recognize all of the constituent parts. In such a case, the learner will presumably have in her or his lexicon both the whole chunk and those parts she or he recognizes, along with some sort of cross-referencing information.

2. A learner may even have been able to identify all the sub-units within some useful larger chunk without being sure enough of the structural pattern to feel confident of being able to reconstruct the chunk from its pieces. Again, for safety's sake it would seem expedient to keep in the lexicon both the large chunk and the sub-units, together with appropriate cross-referencing.

3. A mature language user may find that certain expressions or variations on expressions are so useful that it would be convenient, as a device for conserving processing time and effort, to be able to retrieve them in as prefabricated a form as possible. Such prefabrications could be in either of

two forms: fused and invariant units, and well-rehearsed (automatized) patterns that require a minimum of processing (e.g., in the form of insertion of lexical items into a slot) in order to produce the desired utterance.

This last possibility is consistent with Hayes-Roth's study of "unitization" (1977) which deals with units; Pawley and Syder's exploration of "institutionalized clauses" (1976), which deals with units and frames; and Bisazza's theory of "templating levels" (1978, 78–9), which deals with frames. All three studies are concerned with shortcutting devices in mature or well-learned systems of knowledge (see the discussion in 1.1). In addition, the literature on experimental investigations of the facilitative role of chunking in memory storage and retrieval (see, e.g., Wickelgren 1980) seems to be consistent with the existence of multiple levels of analysis in language.

If we accept, then, that there indeed exist motivations for storage of linguistic units at different levels of analysis, we might ask if there are any neurological observations that are relevant to the notion of multilevel analyses. Recent neurological evidence about the human brain suggests that it has a great deal of memory capacity and powerful information-handling capabilities, but is severely limited in processing speed (Crick, 1979, 219). Redundant forms of storage that would save processing time seem particularly adaptive for such an organ.

Processing time and effort can also be economized through automatization, which Whitaker (1979) defines as the gradual development of a skill into a fast, automatic, and consistent sequence of actions. The literature on automatization of skill learning in other cognitive areas (see, e.g., Anderson 1981) suggests that an extension of this notion to language processing would be appropriate. And, indeed, Whitaker hypothesizes that when a young child is learning language every available neuron is recruited, but that as language skills are refined, a more economical repackaging is effected in a core language area. This hypothesis is based on the fact that early brain damage tends to result in global, rather than specialized, aphasia. On the other hand, random brain damage in an adult is not nearly so likely to affect language, but a focal lesion, even though small, can cause a great deal of damage to the language system. This reduction in the size and concentration of the primary language-processing areas of the brain seems to be due to the automatization of grammatical skills, which enables more efficient language processing. Thus it seems that neurological facts are consistent with the existence of multiple levels of units for adults as well as for children.

Evidence from language use also supports this possibility. In the previous section we saw evidence for the fusion of constructed long units by adults. Further support for automatization appears in the following quotation. Olson suggests that

in performance we are often able to reduce the effective complexity of utterances through the use of preprogrammed routines which represent components of the full description of a sentence as a single label or recoding. For instance, for academicians the subjunctive probably has less effective structural complexity than it does, say, for the hard-hat, since the academician uses it so routinely that it is represented internally as a unitized subroutine rather than as the full set of specific algorithms needed to do the appropriate computation from scratch. [1973, 155]

Barber, in describing the personal experience of trying for the first time to cope with massive doses of spoken Russian, says:

By the third day . . . the linguist in me was noticing a rising din of Russian in my head: words, sounds, intonations, phrases, all swimming about in the voices of the people I talked with . . . The din of sounds in my head became so intense after five days that I found myself mindlessly chewing on them, like so much linguistic cud, to the rhythm of my own footsteps as I walked the streets and museums . . . The constant rehearsal of these phrases of course was making it easier and easier to speak quickly and fluently; things popped out as prefabricated chunks. [1980, 30]

Thus we may need to agree that at least at a performance level there is not a single basic level of lexical units for mature language users. I will explore some of the theoretical consequences of this conclusion in the next chapter. First, however, let us consider how growing automatization benefits the language learner.

As noted by Iwamura (see 3.1.3) and others (MacWhinney 1976, 403; Wong Fillmore 1976), the stress of an urgent attempt to interact verbally, whether to communicate information or to interact socially, may trigger changes in a child's linguistic system to the point at which an observer may hear analyses taking place before her or his very ears. When such communication pressure is considered more closely, it becomes clear that one thing that is often involved is a processing limitation on the part of the child: There is a limit on the availability of resources, such as working memory, information-handling capacity, processing time, and so on, that can be expended in an interaction. In order to concentrate on one aspect of the communication, shortcuts may have to be made in another. Resource-conserving strategies can thus be seen as important concomitants of analytic breakthroughs.

Such resource-conserving strategies include all those devices which we have discussed so far that allow children to say more than their system would otherwise allow: rote memorization of long chunks, buildup of progressively longer utterances, juxtaposition of prefabricated constructions, fusion of often-used sequences, and automatization of often-used processes. Olson also suggests that "the child . . . learns ways to recode portions of [the structure of an utterance] so as to reduce the computational weight associated with longer, more complex utterances" (1973, 156). The resources conserved through using these devices may then be available for unraveling some particularly knotty communicative problem, for instance, the fission of a heretofore unanalyzed chunk and then the synthesis of a part of it into a new construction (see, e.g., Clark's example of *I want Teddy to have a bath* in 4.1.2, and Iwamura's example of *I don't want it to be a shawl* in 3.1.3). Just what this problem is will be determined by the urgency of the particular communication situation. Fission and fusion may thus be seen as complementary strategies as determined by the child's processing limitations.

5   Conclusions and implications

5.1. Theoretical implications

I would like to review eight important points made in this book:

1. The first units of language acquired by children do not necessarily correspond to the minimal units (morphemes) of language described by conventional linguistics. They frequently consist of more than one (adult) word or morpheme.

2. In terms of storage and use, however, there is no difference between such long units and units that happen to be minimal: To the language learner they are all units, and are stored in the lexicon and retrieved as such.

3. All units, or entries, in the learner's lexicon are candidates for the fundamental process of segmentation by which they are broken down into smaller units. Segmentation may be applied to material in ongoing conversations, or to units already stored in the lexicon.

4. The smaller units that result from segmentation are themselves entered in the lexicon.

5. A unit that has been segmented may or may not be deleted from the lexicon: That is, the original unit and the products of segmentation may coexist. [29]

6. Segmentation also results in structural information, beginning with the simplest formulaic frames with slots, which are progressively generalized into more general syntactic patterns. The beginnings of the acquisition of syntax can be observed in this process.

7. The learner's lexicon grows as the learner collects not only units perceived in conversation and the results of their segmentation, but also the results of what I have called fusion (4.2). This is the process by which often-

---

[29] MacWhinney presents an explicit formulation of a model for the acquisition of morphophonology in which alternative representations of an item may be present in the lexicon. He also proposes an explicit feedback cycle that strengthens or weakens a particular representation until presumably only one alternative remains (1978, 12).

89

used combinations are stored as preassembled units for quick and easy retrieval.

8.   The process of fusion continues even into adulthood, where, even though mature speakers have presumably analyzed most of their original lexical entries into ultimate constituents, larger commonly used chunks seem to be available as single fused lexical units in the production of speech. Some items may also be stored at one or more intermediate levels, as partially assembled lexico-syntactic frames with open slots.

What, then, are the theoretical advantages to the linguist of assuming that whole utterances and words are treated in the same ways by the language learner? The biggest gain, to my mind, is in not needing to describe two separate systems.

Another unification made possible by these eight points is the continuity between child and adult language. I will return to this matter, after considering the implications of these points for adult language. Points 5, 7, and 8, in particular, imply that there is considerable redundancy in the storage of both lexical and syntactic information. The relation between syntax and lexicon may therefore be more fluid than is usually supposed: Under some circumstances an expression may be retrieved from the lexicon as a single unit; under others it may be constructed from partially assembled pieces in the lexicon, requiring somewhat more syntactic processing; under yet other circumstances it may be constructed de novo from morphemes. Syntax and lexicon are thus seen to be complementary in a dynamic and redundant way. The same information may be present in both, in different forms: It may be present implicitly in the lexicon fused into an expression or formulaic frame, and at the same time it may be explicitly represented in the syntax.[30]

From the existence of such redundant storage we may infer that storage is not the only parameter that a language user attempts to minimize. Efficiency of processing is an additional, competing requirement. If all lexical and syntactic information were stored without any redundancy, a speaker would have to construct every expression from morphemes. But evidence is accumulating that in order to reduce processing time we indeed use partially redundant forms of storage. This suggests that a realistic theory of language use should incorporate some sort of interaction or tradeoff between storage and processing economy.

---

[30] The formulation of this particular conclusion, though strictly my own, owes a great deal to discussions with Charles Fillmore, John Bisazza, and Andrew Pawley. It is also supported by Bolinger's (1975) observations that "the whole chunks that we learn also persist as coded units even after the chemical anaylsis into words has partially split them up" (1975, 100) and "the brain stores both the parts and the wholes, and we retrieve them when we need them" (105).

Though Occam's razor requires that a description of the structure of a language be free of redundancy, we are here concerned rather with the speaker's knowledge of the language and with the evidence from real speech that this knowledge may actually be stored redundantly. We must account, for instance, for what seem to be alternative ways of producing what from a structural point of view is the same utterance.

Another past motivation for eschewing redundancy has been a misleading analogy that seems to have been drawn between the human brain and early computers. These computers were severely limited in memory capacity, but less limited in computational speed. As we have just seen, however, current evidence about the human brain suggests that it has a great deal of memory capacity (much more than the largest computer available today) and powerful information-handling abilities, but is severely limited in processing speed. Redundant forms of storage that would save processing time seem well adapted for these capabilities.

It seems reasonable and economical to assume that these redundant properties of adult language processing are also present in the child, but merely in different proportions. Although, for the language learner in the very first stages of acquisition, whole utterances may be stored away unanalyzed, they are soon segmented to some extent. As language acquisition proceeds, the proportion of unanalyzed multimorphemic units decreases but probably never entirely vanishes. Thus, even for most adults, there probably remain some potentially analyzable but somewhat opaque items that have not yet been analyzed. This is not to say, however, that the original large chunks are necessarily expunged from storage. In fact, the number of redundantly stored multimorphemic chunks actually would be expected to increase, since often-used constructions can also be stored as fused units, a device used by speakers of all ages. These redundantly stored pieces, however, unlike the large chunks originally learned by the child, are associated with an analysis within the speaker's system; the speaker knows the underlying structure. In studying language acquisition, therefore, we should be aware of (and on the lookout for) this developmental sequence, starting with unanalyzed chunks, proceeding through a stage of more or less complete analysis, and returning to refused but analyzed chunks (see 5.2.1).

A second major implication is that, contrary to the belief implicit in most current research, the learning of syntactic rules is not the first event of structural interest in a child's language acquisition. Rather, the first grammatically significant events are the analyses of individual chunks into shorter recurrent segments and, where a sufficient number of different chunks have been analyzed, the perception of structural patterns.

A corollary is that the role of analogy in language acquisition may be much greater than heretofore acknowledged. Analogy is here defined as the strategy of producing new constructions on the basis of frame- and slot-type patterns that have been discovered through segmentation. This device seems very similar to processes familiar to historical linguists (e.g., Bloomfield 1933; Bolinger 1975), but has been acknowledged as important by very few writers on child language. Although he does not use the term in quite this sense, MacWhinney's use of analogy could be reinterpreted in this light. His model for the acquisition of morphophonology recognizes the need for the child to use not one but three processes that interact in a complex way: "rote memorization, productive combination, and analogical formation" (1978, 1). Here "rote memorization" is roughly equivalent to extraction, "analogical formation" to the use of limited-scope formulas, and "productive combination" to the use of more generalized syntactic patterns. His monograph makes a good case for the importance of analogy in the learning of suffixally inflected languages such as Hungarian and German. Similarly, Berman's data (1981a, b) on the acquisition of Hebrew morphology support the role of analogy in a language where many inflections are sequences of vowels interdigitated with triconsonantal roots. My claim, which follows from the data presented in 3.2 and 4.1, is that this type of analogical processing may be central in the acquisition of syntax as well as of morphology. This is an area that will have to be further explored (see 5.2.1).

Thirdly, we can specify certain cognitive abilities that a child's Language Acquisition System (LAS) would need in order to be able to carry out the acquisition of language along the lines proposed in the eight points with which this chapter opened. As suggested in Chapters 2 and 3, in order to break into the language system the child must have some strategies for extracting manageable chunks of speech from the continuous speech stream, and must be able to remember these chunks for long enough and in enough detail to compare them phonologically, recognize phonetically identical stretches, and remember these, perhaps as well as the residues, as new lexical items. Furthermore, the child must be able to recognize and remember the structural patterns and information about distribution classes revealed by such analysis. As language learning proceeds, the child must be able to utilize lexical and syntactic information already acquired to analyze (parse) new input, as well as be able to revise the lexical and syntactic information already acquired on the basis of new data. In short, a child confronted with an unknown language must use many of the strategies a field linguist would use in a similar situation (see, e.g., Nida 1949).

The set of heuristics presented in this book can be seen as a step toward a model of the earliest perceptual stages of language acquisition. Two specific contributions toward such a model are (1) the marshaling of evidence for a perceptual process in language acquisition in which long units are extracted from heard speech and successively segmented into shorter ones and (2) the demonstration that not only lexical but also syntactic information is gained by the child from such a process of segmentation. These contributions should provide a basis for a more realistic modeling of language acquisition than approaches in which children are assumed to begin with precisely the lexical items of the adult language.

In order to test this model and pursue its implications for language learning, further research focusing on units and their breakdown and absorption into the child's growing lexico-grammatical system will be needed. Such studies will entail coming to grips with the researcher's ability to recognize units in the child's system, as well as the various possible stages of their breakdown (unanalyzed, partially analyzed, fully analyzed, fused). In 1.3.1, I suggested some criteria for distinguishing one-unit from multi-unit utterances. Now, however, we need to be even more sophisticated, since we also need to be able (1) to recognize long units incorporated within multi-unit utterances, and (2) to recognize when they are in the process of breaking down.

Snow has addressed the first of these problems in her investigation of what she calls Expanded Imitations. These include "at least one stressed content word or morpheme from the adult utterance and at least one word or morpheme not in the modelled utterance" (1981a, 207). She proposes that looking at Deferred Imitations, which can occur several hours or even days after the model was heard, will be particularly fruitful in trying to trace the role of imitations in syntactic growth, but concedes that the identification of such imitated chunks poses a serious methodological problem. She offers the following two criteria: "(i) formal, including prosodic, identity to the model, and (ii) initial use in the situation in which the model was heard" (211).

Snow's criteria are similar to those of Moerk and Moerk, who are also concerned with the identification of imitated chunks of language. The differences in the phrasing of their criteria are perhaps useful in a supplementary way. Thus, as their major criterion, they look for "the presence of a largely identical preceding utterance" (1979, 46). As the time span between model and imitation increases, they rely increasingly on probability of occurrence:

The closer the child's utterance followed the model's, identity factors being equal, the higher the probability for it to be classified as imitation. If, however, the construction was very rare or non-existent in the child's normal speech, either in regard to its vocabulary or its syntactic aspect, and if an almost identical model had occurred in the not too distant past, then the child's utterance was defined as imitation in spite of a quite possibly extended temporal interval. [47]

With respect to the second problem raised here, that of identifying units in various stages of breakdown, Moerk and Moerk point out that they found a residue of child utterances for which an unequivocal decision concerning imitative status could not be made: "Known parental models suggested the utterance might be an imitation, but the employed structure was otherwise mastered by the child, so that it could have been formulated spontaneously" (47). But this is just what we should expect if "utterances that were at first obviously imitated . . . are reemployed by the child and are slowly incorporated into his spontaneous repertoire" (47). Thus the criteria for identification of imitations in their initial stages and the expectation that many such imitated chunks may get segmented and absorbed into the child's productive system may be the most important new tools to be added to the researcher's kit at this stage of investigation.

Before going on to suggest specific areas in which research needs to be done I would like to make some comments about the implications of the existence of "long units" for the practice of using mean length of utterance (MLU) as a tool for estimating a child's linguistic competence. To be useful in determining a child's competence, such a metric should presumably measure utterance length in terms of units within the child's linguistic system. In practice, however, it is the number of adult units in the child's utterance that is counted, though even this policy is not followed consistently. I have argued that these are different, the child's units often corresponding to multiple units of the adult system.

As early as 1959 Burling observed:

Most studies of child language put heavy stress on the number of words used in a sentence. This is true of the psychological literature, but it is also true of Leopold's work. My feeling as I observed Stephen's language, and my conclusion now, is that the number of words or morphemes is perhaps the least important criterion of grammatical progress. What from an adult point of view are multi-morphemic words, or multi-word sentences, were used before their complex nature was recognized by Stephen. The most significant single advance in his ability came when he learned to make substitutions, and once this was achieved, he was soon able to make sentences with not just two morphemes but with three and more. One simply cannot reasonably speak of a two-morpheme stage of his speech development. (Since Garo has such complex word formation, it is more significant to consider the number of morphemes in a sentence than the number of words.) [1973, 88]

In spite of these observations, MLU has newly been legitimized, especially among linguists, by Brown's presentation of the rules he used to calculate it for Adam, Eve, and Sarah (1973, 54). These rules seem to have been based on his familiarity with the intuitions about the data from these children, who on the whole seem to have been fairly analytic in their approach to language. There are difficulties, however, with Brown's formulation that may not have been faced by those other workers who, for the sake of comparability, have adopted his rules. These have to do with recognition of what is to be counted as a unit. Brown handles the matter with a set of five rules (numbers 4–8). Thus he decides that all compound words (e.g., *birthday*), proper names, ritualized reduplications (*choo-choo*), irregular past tenses (*got, did*), diminutives (*doggie*), and catenatives (*gonna, wanna*) are to be counted as units since they all seem to function as such for these children. On the other hand, he decides that all auxiliaries and inflections are to be counted as separate morphemes. He overlooks the possibility that the children might not have segmented some of these as separate morphemes – and although this may not have been a problem in Adam's, Eve's and Sarah's uses, it will be in some children's. (At the end of his book he does consider the problem of segmentation as manifested in particular by Adam's *it's* and *that-a* [390–6], but he never relates this difficulty to his early decisions about counting morphemes.) There are also many other potentially unanalyzed chunks that Brown does not deal with in his rules and that have not been adequately considered by subsequent workers attempting to apply these rules. (That is, only the most obvious chunks have been recognized as such, whereas others have generally been dealt with according to the rules of English orthography: If there is a space in the spelling, count two units.) These potential chunks include such common occurrences as *all gone, get up, come here* (*c'mere*), *look at* (*lookit*), and *lie down*.[31]

In short, Brown gives a list of rules of thumb for determining length of utterance based on his inituitive, and probably fairly accurate, feel for what his subjects at the early stages took to be single units. He then suggests that these rules can be used to make "one child's data comparable with another's, one

---

[31] This problem can be seen particularly clearly when one looks at the use of MLU as a measure of development in a morphologically complex language such as American Sign Language (ASL). Thus Terrace et al., state: "In calculating a child's MLU certain conventions are followed that cannot be applied directly to sequences of signs. A spoken utterance, for example, is often broken down into morphemes rather than words: *running* and *run there* would each be regarded as a two-morpheme utterance. In sign language, the utterance, *run there* can be expressed as a single sign . . . One explanation for the apparent delay in the growth of MLU in deaf children has to do with the property of sign language that allows one to encode a number of morphemes within a single sign" (1979, 902). The sign for RUN-THERE, however, though not a sequence of two signs, nevertheless consists of two simultaneously articulated components, the sign RUN plus the path that denotes 'there,' each of which recurs in other signs (Carol Tane Akamatsu, personal communication). The child may or may not be aware of the individual components. If the child is aware, she or he should be given credit for two morphemes in the MLU count. More careful analysis of the morphemic composition of signs and consequent recalculation of MLUs for deaf children may result in the finding that their MLU growth is in fact not delayed with respect to that of hearing children. It may at the same time turn out that MLUs of hearing children have been unduly inflated by the practice of giving them credit for more morphemes than they deserve. Or perhaps it is not valid to compare MLUs across languages of different morphological types.

project with another" (54). It should, however, be evident by now that the usefulness of this technique as a comparative measure is attenuated by the fact that his criteria for what is a unit, developed for Adam, Eve, and Sarah (who were firstborn mainstream American children chosen for their volubility and intelligibility), may not necessarily apply to other children, or to the same children at different stages, or even to the same child in different utterances.

MLU is certainly useful for making rough comparisons among most children learning to speak the same language. But it is also true that for some children, such as Gestalt-oriented ones like Minh, it is virtually impossible to calculate MLU at all. And at finer levels of comparison among children, one needs to be aware of the potential problems in identifying units. Ideally one needs to deal with the problem of what is a unit on a child-by-child, and even utterance-by-utterance, basis. To be able to do this one must first be familiar with both the child's own usage and the language the child hears, in order to be able to recognize recurrent chunks that are likely to be perceived as unitary.

5.2. Further research questions

Although the approach advocated in this book provides a framework within which can be included more of the already observed phenomena of both child and adult speech than has hitherto been possible, it also reveals a number of problems needing more detailed investigation and suggests new areas for research. These problems can be grouped into two main categories: the place of formulaic learning in language acquisition, and the psychological status of various aspects of formulaic speech among adults. In addition, the status of formulaic speech should be explored in two other areas that I will not discuss: the neurolinguistic aspects of formulaic speech and the role in language change of formulaic learning of language. The more detailed questions for the first two categories that I present here are intended to be suggestive rather than exhaustive. Furthermore, since the study of formulaic speech is relatively new to linguistics, it will require some new research methods. Therefore, whenever possible, I also present suggestions about possible approaches to particular problems.

5.2.1. *The role of units in language acquisition*

Studies needed in this area include:

1. Analyses of input speech to see just what sorts of recurrent chunks are available to language learners, coupled with an effort to identify those circumstances under which these chunks are extracted and used by the learners;

2. Collection of evidence on segmentation of large chunks and situations in which segmentation is likely to occur;

3.   Collection of evidence on fusion of large chunks;
4.   A psycholinguistic exploration of what a child perceives to be a unit of language;
5.   An investigation and delimitation of the factors that account for individual differences in the use of large chunks of language;
6.   An investigation of what happens to large recurrent chunks in acquisition of languages of other morphological types than English.

The relation of input speech to extraction.   If extraction of chunks of speech is crucial to language learning, then we should look for the sources of these chunks in the child's environment. This conclusion naturally leads to a new focus for the study of input speech, namely, as a source of chunks to be extracted. Where and when, for instance, is a child most likely to hear recurrent and predictable chunks of speech? A particularly promising place to look would be at family rituals during routine daily activities such as dressing, diapering, bathing, and feeding. Can we document how chunks are extracted and used by children as they learn to participate verbally in such routines? In such studies, both immediate and delayed imitation would constitute evidence of extraction. We would also like to know what sorts of special modifications, such as addition of extra stress, exaggerated intonation contours, or repetition, that are made to input speech result in facilitating the process of extraction of particular chunks.

   In order to carry out such studies, appropriate data collection and research methods will have to be devised. For very young children, well-designed diary studies, such as those proposed in Braunwald and Brislin (1979), will be necessary, since the relevant data will have to include the history of individual chunks picked up by the child – where they came from and what happened to them (both analysis and misanalysis) over a period of time. Such data cannot be collected in one-hour-per-week taping sessions, although judicious use of tape recording will undoubtedly be an important contribution to such studies. In any case, the major part of the data will almost certainly have to be collected by a member or members of the child's family. Since children do seem to show individual differences in picking up and using long chunks, it may be partly a matter of chance whether any particular child will provide much data on formulaic learning and breakdown. Moreover, the sheer intelligibility of a particular child may affect how easy such data are to analyze.

   In addition, we need to know whether adult caretakers are the principal sources of formulaic input for the language learner, or whether older siblings, if present, are also important in this respect. As noted in 2.2.2, Montgomery's study of a pair of sisters showed that the younger had picked up from the older a number of situationally appropriate expressions, "thereby giving illusory impression of advanced competence" (1977, 4). Minh, too, learned such expressions from his older brother, including the useful summons phrase "Mommy, I wanna tell you something," in which the second part was clearly an unanalyzed chunk [āytéiusìnts] when I first heard him use it at 23 months. Input studies, then, need to be extended to include careful assessment of the nature and influence of sibling speech on language acquisition. Furthermore, in cultures where mothers work and institutionalized daycare is common, for example, from age 2½ or 3 in the United States or age 2 in Israel, the language at the daycare center needs to be investigated, not only for ritualized uses, but also for systematic ways in which such routines resemble or differ from routines used at home.

It is also important to look at older children, those beyond the earliest stages of language acquisition. I am convinced that picking up of formulaic chunks is not confined to the earliest stages of language acquisition. For instance, we should examine what I like to call the "out of the mouths of babes" phenomenon, which occurs when an older child startles adults by coming out with a long, extremely mature-sounding and situationally appropriate expression. Under such circumstances the adults typically look at each other and ask, "Where did she get that?" I suspect that many such expressions are picked up without much analysis. A careful diary-type documentation of the history of such expressions would be extremely useful, indicating where they come from, under what circumstances they are used, whether there are misuses that might give clues about incomplete analysis, and so on.

Segmentation of extracted units.   If segmentation of extracted chunks is an important process in language learning, we need to look for evidence of segmentation and the concomitant induction of morpho-syntactic patterns. For instance, as the child's linguistic sophistication grows, one would expect to find more and more instances (within predictable contexts) of expanded imitations of, or variations on, adult utterances. These would constitute evidence that segmentation of the source utterances had indeed taken place. (Again, there might be individual differences among children in the faithfulness, and hence the recognizability, of the imitations.)

We would also like to know what processes might be involved in the extraction of patterns from segmented chunks and their incorporation into the child's growing linguistic system. In particular, what evidence can we find for pattern extraction? Any evidence for the use of analogy in syntax as well as in morphology may be important in this respect. Wong Fillmore's second-language data (1976) are certainly convincing enough to suggest that we should look for analogical processes in first-language acquisition. Whereas MacWhinney (1978) has discussed analogy in the acquisition of morphophonology, the role of this strategy in the acquisition of syntax should now also be investigated. What is crucial is to get enough of the right kind of data to be able to follow the *process* of generalization, from segmentation through limited-scope analogical patterns to more general patterns, along the lines suggested in 3.2.3 and 4.1.

Short of an exhaustive search of a child's entire output, where can we look for such evidence? Again, we should try looking at routines. But whereas it is predictable recurrence that is important for extraction, it is limited variation that will be crucial for segmentation. One research strategy might be to look for interactive routines that would support the acquisition of particular classes of words or specific linguistic constructions. For example, the "What's that?" routine can lead to acquisition of labels, both names and attributes (Ninio & Bruner 1978), and the "Where's your nose?" routine to body-part names (Sachs & Truswell 1978). By the same token, the "What color is this?" routine could be expected to facilitate learning of color words. On a morphological level, we may find that there are routines, such as "Whose X is this?" or "Where is X?" that focus on possessive or locative constructions. Ritual conversations such as "Where's daddy? He's gone to work" may perhaps serve as models, not only for learning to talk about displaced reference (i.e., what needs to be specified in order to identify absent people or past events [Cazden 1979, 12]), but also for learning the syntax necessary for such talk (Stoel-Gammon & Cabral 1977).

Another approach is to look for routines that operate in the dual contexts of communicative functions and linguistic socialization. That is, what kinds of communicative functions do children have to acquire (such as greeting, leave-taking, requesting, thanking, interrupting, asking for information, giving information), and what are the ways in which they are taught to carry out these functions? (see the discussions in Gleason & Weintraub 1978; Schieffelin 1979). In particular, in what ways might linguistic routines be used to scaffold such learning? Also, if the child's ability to imitate modeled utterances is central in such routines, how is the expectation of imitation taught to the child? Do the routines for teaching such communicative functions change with the age of the child – one routine, for example, being used with babies but being dropped in favor of another as the child becomes a toddler?[32] And, most crucial for our purposes, how is variation introduced and the range of acceptable variation conveyed?

For older children, too, such as the 3-year-olds studied by Iwamura and the school-age children studied by Wong Fillmore, there is evidence that the children's strong desire to communicate with each other may have catalyzed both the picking up of chunks and their subsequent segmentation. This suggests that

---

This last question arises from preliminary results of research conducted by Karen Watson-Gegeo in the Solomon Islands (personal communication).

settings where children are highly motivated to communicate – child–child conversations, for example, as opposed to adult–child interviews – may be particularly fruitful sources of data.

Fusion of large chunks.   We also need more information about the processes by which useful chunks are built up and fused. In particular, since morphophonemic processes seem to be highly automatized in mature speakers of a language, it would be particularly enlightening to document how they get this way. MacWhinney (1978) has already detailed two stages of acquisition of morphophonology: (1) "rote memorization," where inflections are not yet recognized as separate elements and mistakes of construction do not occur; and (2) the early stages of synthesis, which MacWhinney divides into "analogical formation" and "productive combination" and which are characterized by errors of overgeneralization. I believe these (intermediate) stages should also be characterized by signs of relatively laborious production and by concomitant reduction in processing capacity available to other tasks in utterance production. As automatization develops and fusion progresses, these signs of difficulty should disappear. This final stage, then, should be characterized by smooth production, lack of hesitations or self-corrections, absence of analogical or combinational errors, evidence of more processing devoted to other aspects of production, and automatic morphophonemic adjustments when speech errors occur.[33]

Iwamura (1980) has some pertinent data, for a more advanced stage of grammatical development, on negotiation and subsequent fusion of what might be called compound words (see the "no–yes" and "down-floor-dress" examples in 4.2.2). Note that such fusions are not necessarily absolute, in the sense that an often-used phrase may at some times be more unitary than at others. Evidence for this can be seen in variable points for the application of inflections, as when a colleague of mine recently said "point of views" and in the next clause "points of view" (and when questioned afterward confessed to having been unaware of the variation he had produced). In fact, I suspect that a succession of stages in the automatization of grammatical processes above the word could also be documented if they were looked for (see, e.g., Johnson's 1980 study on question words). These sorts of data would substantiate Bisazza's (1978) claims about the existence of a number of different "Templating Levels," as discussed in 1.1. I can offer an anecdote that suggests what one might look for in the way of such evidence: I remember my son going through several stages of what seemed to me to be incipient stutter

---

[33] An example of this last is the voicing adjustment in "both sicks are kid" (for the intended "both kids are sick"). This example and other similar ones can be found in Fromkin 1973, 258–9.

ing at around age 3. Each time I was very worried, but after a week or so the difficulty would iron itself out, and I would notice that he was now producing syntactically more complex sentences. Unfortunately, I did not keep a diary of the exact gains he made, but these would be the kinds of data to look for.

Another possible source of data on fusion that would be worth exploring is the evolution of narratives that get told more than once, as when a child reports an event right after it happens and sometime later is asked to repeat the narrative to a new audience. In the first telling the child would be struggling to find ways to report the salient events. These struggles, aided by promptings, questionings, and clarifications from the first audience, would serve as a rehearsal for the second telling, which could be expected to be smoother and more effective. An example of such a repeated narrative can be found in Halliday (1975, 112). In my own data I have only the second story in such a sequence. At the time of the first telling, the 4-year-old narrator's father had been struck by the difficulty the boy was having in reporting the event, so the next day the father asked his son to tell me the story. This time, to the surprise of the father, the story was told relatively smoothly and easily.

The child's conception of a "word."   Several studies have attempted to investigate children's conceptions of what a word is by asking them to indicate the number of words in given sentences (see, e.g., Berthoud-Papandropolou 1978; Lawler 1976). Both Lawler and Berthoud-Papandropolou, working respectively in English and French, found what Lawler calls the "functor effect" (2), whereby functors are not accorded the status of words by preschoolers, although nouns and verbs are. But in neither study was an attempt made to investigate systematically the question whether commonly occurring phrases would be more likely to be accorded single-"word" status than more obviously constructed phrases. For instance, given the sentences "It was a bright sunny morning" and "Mr. Jones said, 'Good morning,'" would *good morning* be perceived as more unitary than *sunny morning*? Such a study would provide evidence regarding one of the fundamental claims of this book, namely, that children's units are not necessarily the same as linguists'.

Individual differences.   Evidence is accumulating that children do not all follow the same paths on the way to language acquisition – at least with respect to the kinds of utterances they produce. What goes on in their minds is another question, but one to which we can only infer the answers. Certainly, some children talk more than others, or are more intelligible, or are more adventuresome (as opposed to conservative) with language, or rely more on readily identifiable patterns (e.g., limited-scope formulas). Therefore we need more documentation on these different overt manifestations of the ranges of strategies children can use in their move toward adult language. And we need to try to make whatever links we can between these strategies and the factors that may foster them, such as those proposed in 2.2 and 3.4. But we must bear in mind that just because a child does not overtly use a particular strategy (e.g., imitate a great deal), it does not necessarily imply that she or he is not using the strategy covertly. Rather, in such an instance we can only say that we have no evidence about what is going on in the child's head.

The contributing factors proposed in 2.2 and 3.4 can be divided into two types: those internal to and those external to the child. Internal factors include individual neurological endowment (2.2.4); external factors include aspects of input, language use, and cultural expectations, including tolerance for large chunks and amount and variability of routines. It seems, then, not only that we need to collect more data on individual differences with respect to the extraction, segmentation, and fusion of linguistic chunks, but that such data need to be focused in two different ways: We need data to point up individual differences within a culture, and we need data on acquisition under different cultural conditions.

Languages of different morphological types.   Not only do we need to know more about language acquisition under different cultural conditions, we also lack information about linguistic development in languages of other morphological types than English, especially at the early stages. We particularly need to know more about how children go about solving extraction and segmentation problems in diverse languages, since certain properties of a language will affect how easy or hard it is to accomplish these tasks (see Peters 1981 for a somewhat more detailed discussion of the questions presented in this section). For example, the fact that English is a stress-timed language makes it relatively difficult for the learner to perceive functors as separate units, since they tend to be phonologically inconspicuous. The unpredictable position of stress within English words can also be expected to contribute to difficulty in recognition of word boundaries (see, for example, the word-boundary shifts in the misperceptions and misanalyses discussed in Chapter 3). Similarly, in languages with cliticization and elision, such as French, where phonological and lexical words do not coincide very well, one would also expect children to have word-boundary problems. This expectation is supported by Grégoire's description of the difficulty French children have in determining the initial phoneme of words that begin with vowels. He cites the example of a 2-year-old boy who makes a number of attempts at saying the word *arbre* 'tree', each time picking up a different elided initial consonant: *le beau z-abe, le beau t-arbe, un petit n-arpe, au l'arpe* (1971, 94). In the same vein, Guillaume gives examples of cliticized pronouns' being perceived as integral parts of verbs beginning with vowels: *Tu la l'ôtes, Moi la l'ai vue, Il la l'ouvre* (1973a, 242).

Even though English may present some difficulties in word-boundary recognition, it has relatively little word-internal morphology to be learned, especially before the latinate vocabulary begins to be acquired. This situation contrasts with that presented by highly inflecting languages. In those languages where there is "heavy" sandhi (such as metathesis, epenthesis, deletion, diphthongization, or fusion of vowels) at morpheme boundaries, segmentation will be correspondingly harder than in highly agglutinative languages with no sandhi at the boundaries. Some evidence for the problems caused by opaque morphophonemics comes from Hungarian, where word-internal morphophonemic processes make it relatively difficult to separate stems from affixes (MacWhinney 1978), and French, where the learning of the verb-conjugation system presents a number of problems (Guillaume 1973a). On the other hand, children seem to have little difficulty in finding morpheme boundaries in such agglutinative languages as Turkish (Ekmeci 1979; Slobin & Aksu 1980) and SiSwati (Kunene 1979). Besides degree of morphophonemic opacity, other variables that may affect segmentability of affixes are their syllabicity (or lack thereof), stressability, and consistency of form (see Pye 1980 for discussion and examples from Quiche Mayan).

In Semitic languages, which are characterized by interdigitated roots and inflections, children are faced with an entirely different kind of problem. Here they have no segmentation clues other than similarity of patterning to guide them to the realization of how roots and inflections must be disentangled, and at first they have no choice but to memorize inflected forms as units. Eventually, however, they will have built up a large enough corpus of memorized forms so that when they line them up mentally they will be able to perceive the inflectional patterns and extract the roots. See Berman (1981a) for a detailed discussion, including difficulties Israeli children have with certain opaque roots. In all of these morphologically complex languages, the role of analogy in language acquisition may be greater than it is in English.

In polysynthetic languages, where morphological structure is much more opaque, children may be faced with the choice of either memorizing entire words or extracting the most phonologically salient parts of words (e.g., the stressed parts and/or the ends). What role analogy would have in the subsequent breaking down of such large chunks as get extracted is not at all clear. We do not even know how much morphological segmentation is accomplished by the mature speakers of such languages. This is an area of child language acquisition and psycholinguistics in which we have even fewer data than we have for other language types. Another intriguing question relating to the acquisition of polysynthetic languages concerns the kinds of possible help caretakers might provide. Whereas in isolating and inflecting languages caretakers may present morpho-syntactic minimal pairs (via expansions and reductions of previous utterances) that serve to help the child with phonological comparison and factoring, it is not yet known whether this kind of help is even possible for polysynthetic languages.

Another reason for studying the acquisition of languages of differing structural types is that in limiting ourselves almost exclusively to a heavily syntax-oriented language, namely, English, we have been led to a much stronger focus on acquisition of syntax than on acquisition of morphology. Languages of the world, however, vary in the amount of functional weight borne by syntax and morphology. The way this weight is distributed in a particular language should affect what parts of the system children must learn first in order to be able to communicate their needs. Thus, if Brown (1973) is right in claiming that there are certain semantic relations that children tend to express early, children will first have to learn that part of the grammar (whether it is morphology or syntax or a mixture) which will allow them to express those relations. Burling, in fact, has already called attention to the possibility that in some languages morphology may be more important in early language acquisition than is customarily acknowledged:

It has generally been assumed that syntactical constructions precede morphological ones. Leopold states baldly, "In the field of grammar, syntax comes before morphology. The student of child language becomes very conscious of the fact that the morphological devices are a luxury of fully developed languages. The small child gets along quite well without them, for a short or long time." It is difficult and perhaps arbitrary in many languages to draw the line between morphology and syntax, but it is extremely convenient to make such a distinction for Garo, since there are stretches of several syllables set off by characteristic junctures which can be called words, and the grammatical devices used to form these words are very different from those used to join words together. If the distinction is made, Stephen defied the generalization that syntax comes first by learning to make both types of constructions simultaneously. Some reasons for this are obvious: What I am calling morphology in Garo is much more essential than the morphological process of English, or even of the other European languages. Morphology is not a "luxury" of the fully developed language. Moreover, it is far more regular, and therefore no doubt easier to learn than the morphology of European languages. [1973, 88–9]

In early acquisition of morphology, fission and fusion processes might have an even more important role than in the acquisition of syntax, since words, the raw material for morphological analysis, being typically more phonologically unified than phrases, may be more readily perceived and stored as unanalyzed chunks.

Finally, it would be revealing to look at data on acquisition of American Sign Language (ASL) for insights into how children go about handling simultaneous (as opposed to sequential) complexity. For instance, aspect, number, path of movement, various classifiers, and reference to origin and goal can all be incorporated into ASL verbs, giving rise to morphologically very complex signs (Fischer & Gough 1978; Newport 1981). How are these perceived by children and how do the children go about sorting out the components? At the earliest stages complex signs may be perceived as unanalyzed wholes. For instance, one child who wanted her mother to look at her signed I-LOOKAT-YOU instead of YOU-LOOKAT-ME,[34] where the difference between these two sign complexes is merely one of hand orientation. In this instance the child could have copied what she actually signed directly from her mother as a single unanalyzed unit (see the similar verbal examples presented in 1.3.1, in which the pronouns were not yet being treated as replaceable morphemes: e.g., *Sit my knee*).

Although the studies of the acquisition of ASL that I have seen have dealt with children of 2½ or older (thus presumably well beyond the initial extraction stage), there is a little support for the unanalyzed-chunk hypothesis in Newport's study of the acquisition of ASL verbs by three children. At the first session the youngest child, who was 2;4, produced two correct complex signs (out of a total of ten movement signs elicited during that session), whereas from 2;6 through 2;9 she produced no correct complex signs but seven with missing morphemes (out of a total of sixteen elicited [Newport 1981, tab. 2]). These results would be consistent with a preliminary stage of extracting unanalyzed complex signs, followed by a further extraction of some but not all of the component morphemes.

Another interesting question relating to the acquisition of ASL concerns the place of recurrent finger-spelled sequences. At what point, if ever, is finger spelling separated out as a subsystem of ASL? How is it perceived and used by preschool signers? How, if ever, is it eventually related to the written alphabet? Perhaps a better understanding of these processes would help in teaching deaf children to read.[35]

5.2.2. *The psycholinguistic status of formulaic chunks for adults*

In order better to understand the place of formulaic chunks in children's developing language systems, we need a better understanding of the status of

---

[34] Susan Fischer, personal communication.
[35] Akamatso (1982) is a recently completed dissertation on this topic.

formulaic chunks in adult speech (i.e., a better understanding of what the children's systems can be expected to develop into). In particular, if, as suggested in 5.1, there is indeed a relationship between syntax and lexicon that is both redundant and fluid, we need more evidence of the exact nature of this relationship. Some linguists (e.g., Fillmore 1978; Nagy 1978) have already shown that in order to account for the linguistic constraints on certain English constructions, these constructions must be stored in some sort of phraseological way in any lexical model. Such constructions include not only idioms, which are the most wordlike in their arbitrariness and lack of analyzability (Nagy 1978, 289), but also figures of speech, clichés, and collocations that, although more analyzable than idioms, are nevertheless somewhat "transformationally deficient" (Nagy 1978, 291) (see also the discussion in 1.1). To complement the continuing efforts to describe these sorts of phraseological units, I would like to suggest several sorts of investigations that could be carried out on adult language.

We need to study the range of variability in size of adult linguistic units in order to answer questions such as how the size of units varies. This matter could be investigated under both naturalistic and experimental conditions. Let us first look at ways in which naturally occurring data could be collected. One way would be to collect specific kinds of speech errors similar to those given by Fromkin (1973). One relevant kind of "error" would involve variability in the points at which inflectional affixes could be applied, as in the "point of views" example cited in 5.2.1. Another type of speech error, which I call a "crossed collocation," also gives evidence of formulaic processing. Such errors are similar to the word-level speech errors known as "blends" (e.g., *momentary* + *instantaneous* > *momentaneous*, or *mainly* + *mostly* > *maistly* [Fromkin 1973, 260]), except that they involve the blending of two semantically similar multi-word phrases that are also syntactically similar enough so that the speaker can get derailed from one to the other. Some documented examples will illustrate this phenomenon:[36]

He was breathing down my neck.
He was looking over my shoulder. } He was breathing down my shoulder.

I stuck my neck out.
I went out on a limb. } I stuck my neck out on a limb.

In one ear and out the other.
Here today and gone tomorrow. } In one ear and gone tomorrow.

Notice in each case that the two original expressions share a common word where the derailment can occur. The fact that phrases such as *breathing down*

---

[36] These examples were reported to me by Andrew Pawley, Charles Fillmore, and Victoria Fromkin, respectively. I myself have independently observed an instance of the first example.

my neck and *looking over my shoulder* can be subject to the same sort of retrieval error as single words like *mainly* and *mostly* gives us another clue that these phrases might at least sometimes be stored and retrieved much as single words are.

Another useful study would be a look at adult grammatical errors for evidence of formulaic processing and misanalysis. College or community college English compositions or term papers might be fruitful sources of such data. An example of the type of thing to look for is the not uncommon rendering of *would've* as *would of* rather than *would have*. Guillaume (1973b, 523–5) has collected a large number of such examples from the correspondence of French adults, including cases of running words together, for example, *ai dit* > *aidi*, *est-ce que* > *esque*, *s'est mis* > *semy;* oversegmentation of words, for example, *assez* > *a ses*, *trouvais* > *trou vais*, *encore* > *en core;* and combinations of these two, for example, *j'apprend* > *ja prend*, *d'école* > *dé colle*. Once a list of common formulaic misanalyses had been collected, one could use them as a basis for eliciting further information about their status in adult language systems, for example, by embedding them in sentences to be dictated, asking subjects to explain their structure, and so on. Needless to say, the subject population would have to consist of nonlinguists!

For literate speakers of languages that use the orthographic convention of spaces to indicate word breaks, learning to read marks the point at which knowledge of written forms begins to influence speakers' decisions about word boundaries. Therefore an investigation of perception of word (unit) boundaries among adults who do not write with word breaks would be very revealing.[37] Subjects in such studies might be illiterates, persons whose writing system does not conventionally indicate word breaks, or those whose language is not widely written (e.g., ASL). Interesting questions to ask would include: What sorts of units do particular subjects recognize? How much intersubject variability is there? How are such judgments affected by various types of context, including how the instructions are given? In particular, to what extent do linguistically naive signers recognize the componential nature of signs such as RUN-THERE, I-LOOKAT-YOU, CAR-TURN-CORNER? There is some evidence from signers' "slips of the hand" that these components are functionally independent in that an error can be made in just one morpheme of a complex (multimorphemic) sign (Newkirk, et al. 1980). How conscious signers are of these separate morphemes would be a matter for further psycholinguistic investigation.

Experimental investigation of unit size could include (1) having subjects indi-

---

[37] A look at subjects' decisions about how to write unfamiliar compound words for which word-spacing conventions have not been standardized might also tell something about how many units each compound is thought to consist of. Thanks for this idea are due to Nancy Dorian (personal communication).

cate "units" via finger tapping (once per unit, but one would have to be careful how the instructions were worded), or (2) tachistoscopic recognition times for high-frequency versus low-frequency phrases (controlling both for number of letters and for number of word spaces). Along this line, van Lancker and Canter (1981) have begun investigating the circumstances under which idiomatic phrases may be interpreted literally as opposed to idiomatically.

Since the very nature of formulaic speech processing has to do with words embedded in large contexts, still more work needs to be done on perception of fluent running speech. What sorts of segmentation cues do adults use? What are the respective roles of phonetic saliency (stress, pitch, clearness of articulation), semantics (lexical retrieval and semantic expectations), and syntax (expectations of certain syntactic constructions)? As a start, Clark and Clark (1977, 210–19) report on some interesting instrumental techniques that have been used to approach some of these questions. Is the account of misperceptions presented in 3.3 indeed correct? If not, how should it be altered? Can we investigate the conditions under which a hearer, when presented with the beginning of a possible formula, is likely to expect the formula rather than an analytic construction? Van Lancker, Canter, and Terbeek (1981) have made a start at answering this last question by looking at the phonetic cues supplied by speakers who are asked to produce "ditropic" sentence pairs (i.e., those which, like "He didn't know he was skating on thin ice," can be interpreted either idiomatically or non-idiomatically) so as to convey the two possible readings as clearly as possible. It was found that under these conditions speakers tend to increase the length of and the pauses between the main words in producing the nonidiomatic versions, while running the idiomatic versions together into more holistic units.

Another kind of study that it should be possible to conduct would be documentation of the progress of formulaic synthesis and fusion in technical jargon and ingroup language. Groups of people who share a great deal of knowledge and who interact regularly, such as groups of colleagues or inti-mate groups of friends, regularly negotiate new uses of language with which to talk about new ideas and/or events. At first such language may be laboriously constructive, but as both the constructions and the meanings become established, shortcuts are taken until conveniently brief new expressions have evolved (much as in Suzy and Nani's "down-floor-dress" example in 4.4.2). Diary studies of colleagues' work sessions could reveal the steps in this process, and tape recording and phonetic analysis of such expressions at various stages of fusion might give us phonetic clues to help determine the state of fusion of other expressions of unknown history.

Another interesting way to observe fusion in action is to study the evolu-tion of an oral narrative. Whereas Labov (1972) focused on the syntactic devices that make for an effectively told story, the study suggested here would trace the increasing effectiveness of such a story through repeated tellings. The kind of story to trace is the narration of a repeatedly "reportable" (in the sense of Labov 1972, 370–1) event, such as one resulting in a visible injury (large bandage, cast on arm or leg), which repeatedly elicits the question "What happened to you?" Presumably the answer to such a question would go through a series of stages, since at each telling the speaker would modify the story according to audience reaction, striving each time for a more effective account (until such time as boredom with the whole affair set in, with a resulting tendency for the account to be abbreviated). As the narrator evolved effective ways of conveying the various details of the story, I would expect to find fusion of the phrases used to recount those details, which would allow constructional effort to be shifted to the expression of other aspects of the story (see the discussion of processing limitations in 4.3).

5.3. Some practical implications

Besides the rather basic linguistic and psycholinguistic research questions I have been proposing in this chapter, what are the immediate practical implications for areas such as second-language teaching, bilingual classrooms, or language therapy? On the most superficial level it might seem that the case I have been making for the importance to the learner of large chunks of language could be taken as support for advocating a return to old-fashioned pattern practice. This is not precisely the case: Although I think that there are indications that certain kinds of work with linguistic routines will prove useful in a number of teaching situations, these routines will need to be handled in a much more sophisticated fashion than in pattern practice.

As I have already noted in Chapter 1 (1.3.2), there is a pedagogical bias against the idea of rote memorization of long chunks of speech.[38] Thus Krashen and Scarcella (1978) argue that such long chunks are of little use either in real-life conversations or in the acquisition of grammar. Pattern drill exercises, where substitutions are made within formulaic frames, are also objected to on the grounds that they are so mindless that they are ineffective in promoting real second-language learning (see Lamendella 1979). It is

---

[38] This bias is partly motivated by theoretical considerations, particularly reaction against behavioristic (stimulus–response) models of language learning. But there may be unconscious cultural influences here, too, in that in the United States we tend to look down on imitation as being somehow inferior to processes that are seen as creative. This contrasts with, for instance, the attitude of the Chinese, who highly value memorization and see it as a powerful means of acquiring all kinds of knowledge. I am grateful to Claudine Poggi and Theodore Rodgers for this insight. For a view of how one Chinese mother encourages her daughter's use of linguistic imitation, see Poggi (1982).

indeed true that memorization of long chunks of speech (e.g., individual sentences in a dialogue) is at its simplest the equivalent of memorizing so many long "words," but only if no grammatical analysis (e.g., segmentation) is ever performed on these items. Since the likelihood of needing any of these exact "words" is quite small, such a procedure seems to be a relatively profitless way of cluttering up the memory of a student, who would be better off learning to construct more useful sentences.

Nevertheless, though many of the objections to memorization and pattern practice are valid, there are also advantages (to these or related activities) that should not be thrown out with the bath water. Thus memorization and pronunciation practice of long chunks do at least allow the learner to concentrate on fluent phonological production of relatively long pieces in a situation where other aspects of the processing load have been minimized. There is some evidence that second-language learners in naturalistic situations spontaneously rehearse phrases they have extracted and memorized; see, for instance, the quotation in 4.3 regarding Barber's experience (1980) with Russian. Although such practice may be effective in increasing fluency, it should not be overused to the point of boredom, and it must be combined with complementary teaching techniques involving use of the sentences in meaningful situations, as well as presentation of opportunities to do grammatical analysis on the sentences (there is further discussion of this matter later in the chapter). The biggest problem, then, with merely memorizing phrases and sentences lies in the fact that no systematic support is provided for segmenting these chunks and relating their structural patterns to patterns that are already known.

Are substitution drills, which do involve working with simple patterns, any better in this regard? One strike against them is that, as Lamendella claims, they can be performed completely mindlessly, utilizing only what he calls the "speech copying circuits" (1979, 14). Nevertheless, such drills can also be used as a way of gaining fluency in elementary construction (synthesis) and of consolidating partially learned patterns in a situation where other aspects of the processing load are reduced. Again, learners outside formal learning situations may spontaneously engage in such patterned rehearsals. Consider the following examples from Wong Fillmore:

(While getting settled for the March 12, 1980 ESL lesson, Tony suddenly begins reciting to himself. He gets louder and louder as he does:)

What is that? That is a dok (dog)!
What is that? That is a baseball.
What is that? That is a telephone.
What is that? That is a robin.
    (Etc., etc., for 33 turns, including the following:)

What is that? That is a teenage queen!
What is that? That is a you.
What is that? That is a alphabet.
What is that? That is a Eleanore.

(On the day of the observations, another child recited a litany of apologies to himself as he worked on his math paper:)

I'm solly, William.
I'm solly, James.
I'm solly, Tony . . .   [1980, 16]

One pedagogical challenge, then, would seem to be to use such drills just enough to promote fluency and confidence without overdoing them in the direction of mindless exercise.

But memorizing large chunks and working with simple presegmented patterns, useful as they may be in developing fluency, are only small steps toward the larger goals of free creativity in language use. The implications of this book are that one way to accomplish this goal might be by encouraging the learner to segment known chunks and to extract and begin to use the associated structural patterns. In support of such an approach, there is plenty of evidence from studies of naturalistic second-language learning, such as those of Huang and Hatch (1978), Vihman (1979), and Wong Fillmore (1976), that children often do just this, starting by extracting large chunks that they then segment into smaller pieces. Such a method is also consistent with recent developments in language teaching, such as communicative language teaching (see, e.g., Littlewood 1981) or the notional-functional approach (see, e.g., Wilkins 1976), where the emphasis is on routines and formulas needed to perform specific speech "functions."

Can spontaneous segmentation be fostered in the classroom? I believe it can, but first we need to do more psycholinguistic research to determine at what point in its learning a unit is most segmentable. In the initial stages of learning a chunk, the phonetic details tend not to be very clearly perceived; it is hard enough at this point just to recognize or pronounce the chunk, without having to worry about how it has been constructed. On the other hand, once a chunk has been very well learned (or "overlearned"), it may already have undergone certain processes of automatization (through much rehearsal) to the point where it is somehow fossilized as a unit. By this stage it may no longer be easy to segment. This conclusion would fit with observations (such as those made by Brown & Hanlon 1970, 51, quoted in 1.3.2; or by Clark 1977, 344, quoted in 4.1.1) that in language acquisition items learned as chunks tend to persist as such and to resist segmentation. Rather than doing as others have done and adducing this phenomenon as evidence that segmentation of acquired chunks is not important in second-language learning, I would suggest that we look for an optimal segmentation period at an earlier stage of learning. I would predict that segmentation would be catalyzed by introducing controlled variation within learned chunks just at the point where they have been well enough learned so that resources are freed for paying attention to structure, but before they have been so well learned as to be automatized (see, for instance, Roger Brown's description of his successful segmentation of *korewa*, quoted in 3.1.2). Thus it would seem that students would need as data small sets of related utterances on which to do phonological comparison and factoring, and also some sort of motivation to perform that analysis. Given such data, learners are in a position actually to construct their own grammar in personally meaningful ways, rather than having it fed in pre-determined spoonfuls for which they may not be ready.

Other factors affecting the likelihood of segmentation may be rather socio-linguistic. Thus Wong Fillmore's work (1976, 1979) has shown that for children social meaningfulness is an extremely important factor, and Iwamura's work with first-language learners (1980) points up the role of communicative stress (i.e., really wanting to say something meaningful and straining all resources to do it). Ferguson (1976, 141) gives a nice anecdote relating how, under a certain amount of social pressure to speak, he was able to construct a socially appropri-ate and grammatically acceptable reply in Arabic to a formulaic congratulation he had never heard before. He did this by analyzing the new formula by analogy with similar formulas he already knew, and extracting the root, which he then used to construct the reply on the pattern of familiar associated replies. It is just this sort of exercise, based on taking apart already memorized chunks and putting them together again in new ways, that should give students maximal opportunity to build their own grammars.

Once we learn when and how segmentation can be triggered, we will be in a position to take advantage of language users' natural abilities and tendencies to assign whatever structure they can to stretches of speech, regardless of how much sense can be made of them. (That even adults do this actively and naturally as a matter of course can be seen from the prevalence, in the presence of noise, of mishearings, misanalyses, and even reanalyses, as discussed in 3.3.) The goal, then, would be to design a set of materials that would lead the learners to perform their own segmentation and actively construct their own grammar, rather than having it spoonfed by teacher or textbook. Such materials could present the raw ingredients for grammar building in a much less haphazard sequence than would be likely to occur in a total-immersion situation, and would thus allow students to build up their grammar in a systematic fashion. On the other hand, this procedure would suffer from lack of the pressures of the real-world communication situa-tion, unless they could somehow be incorporated in the teaching technique.

Points from this book that might prove to be of practical use include the following:

1.   Invariant formulas or routines are likely to become automatized, and thus frozen (as well as boring, since they offer no further challenge to the learner once memorized).
2.   The introduction of controlled variation within learned but not yet automatized formulas or routines may be a way to foster segmentation and pattern extraction.
3.   Encouragement of expanded and varied imitations may be a particularly useful technique for consolidating new patterns, as well as for fostering diffusion of these patterns into new contexts.
4.   Individuals and cultures differ in their tolerance for big as opposed to small chunks of language.
5.   The"scaffolding" principle discussed in 3.4.3 might be a useful concept around which to design routines that would encourage learners to do their own segmentation. At first glance it would seem easier to develop such teaching routines for one-on-one situations like individual tutoring or language therapy than for large groups. I think, however, that, keeping the following points in mind, it should be possible to develop scaffolded routines for classroom use as well. What is needed at first is a single, very predictable situation, perhaps focused on a needed communicative function, along with some sort of fixed phrase or set of phrases for dealing with that situation.[39] Once this language has been fairly well learned, variation can be introduced in the form of several types of rephrasings, including expansions and reductions as well as variations and substitutions (see 3.4.2). Situational support will still be available for understanding these new forms, since they will all be centered around the original context. The variations offered should be systematic enough to foster segmentation and pattern perception. Accordingly, the goal would be to introduce sets of utterances that are both functionally and syntactically related – a kind of theme and variations, where the range of variation broadens with the increasing sophistication of the learner. As the learners note these variations they can be encouraged to produce similar variations of their own, thereby consolidating the patterns they have perceived.

5.4. Conclusion

As must have been evident at various points in this presentation and particularly in this chapter, I have been able only to sketch the outlines of a theory of early language acquisition, while leaving large patches of it unexplored. This being the case, it is inappropriate to offer any formal "conclusion": We are

---

[39] Again, recent teaching methods are focusing on building lessons around specific communicative needs, such as getting into and out of conversations, introducing new topics, requesting information, answering questions. I would venture further, suggesting that segmentation can also be fostered in such situations.

only at the outset of a newly defined course of exploration. But if there is any single concept that I would like most to leave with the reader it is this, that we must approach the study of language acquisition from the child's point of view, being aware of and trying to avoid any preconceptions derived from the linguist's description of the adult language system. Only from observations that are interpreted on the basis of this principle can we justify inferences about the processes of language acquisition. Although the mechanisms presented in this book may need to be modified, or even in some cases replaced in the light of further observations, this basic principle must still be the guide to interpreting the observations.

References

Akamatsu, Carol Tane. The acquisition of fingerspelling in preschool children. Doctoral dissertation, University of Rochester, 1982.

Anderson, John R. (Ed.). *Cognitive Skills and Their Acquisition*. Hillsdale, N.J.: Erlbaum, 1981.

Barber, E. J. W. *Archaeological Decipherment*. Princeton: Princeton University Press, 1974.

Barber, E. J. W. Language acquisition and applied linguistics. *ADFL Bulletin*, 1980, *12*, 26–32.

Bateson, Mary Catherine. Linguistic models in the study of joint performances. In M. D. Kinkade, K. L. Hale, and O. Werner (Eds.), *Linguistics and Anthropology: In Honor of C. F. Voegelin*. Lisse: Peter de Ridder Press, 1975.

Bauman, Richard, and Joel Sherzer (Eds.). *Explorations in the Ethnography of Speaking*. Cambridge: Cambridge University Press, 1974.

Berko, Jean. The child's learning of English morphology. *Word*, 1958, *14*, 150–77.

Berman, Ruth Aronson. Early verbs: comments on how and why a child uses his first words. *International Journal of Psycholinguistics*, 1978, *5*, 21–39.

Berman, Ruth Aronson. Regularity vs anomaly: the acquisition of Hebrew inflectional morphology. *Journal of Child Language*, 1981a, *8*, 265–82.

Berman, Ruth Aronson. Acquisition of Hebrew. Manuscript (first draft), University of Tel-Aviv, 1981b.

Berthoud-Papandropolou, Ioanna. An experimental study of children's ideas about language. In A. Sinclair, R. J. Jarvella, and W. J. M. Levelt (Eds.), *The Child's Conception of Language*. New York: Springer-Verlag, 1978.

Bisazza, John. The structure of linguistic competence: templates for verbal behavior. Manuscript, University of Hawaii, 1978.

Bloom, Lois. *Language Development: Form and Function in Emerging Grammars*. Cambridge, Mass.: MIT Press, 1970.

Bloom, Lois. *One Word at a Time*. The Hague: Mouton, 1973.

Bloom, Lois, Patsy Lightbown, and Lois Hood. Structure and variation in child language. *Monographs of the Society for Research in Child Development*, 1975, *40*(2, Serial No. 160).

Bloomfield, Leonard. *Language*. New York: Holt, Rinehart & Winston, 1933.

Blount, Ben G. Aspects of Luo socialization. *Language in Society*, 1972, *1*, 235–48.

Bolinger, Dwight. *Aspects of Language* (2nd ed.). New York: Harcourt Brace Jovanovich, 1975.

Bolinger, Dwight. Meaning and memory. *Forum Linguisticum*, 1976, *1*(1), 1–14.

Braine, Martin D. S. On learning the grammatical order of words. *Psychological Review*, 1963, *70*, 323–48.

Braine, Martin D. S. On two types of models in the internalization of grammars. In Dan I. Slobin (Ed.), *The Ontogenesis of Grammar*. New York: Academic Press, 1971.

Braine, Martin D. S. Children's first word combinations. *Monographs of the Society for Research in Child Development*, 1976, *41*(1, Serial No. 164).

115

Branigan, George, and William Stokes. An integrated account of utterance variability in early language development. Paper presented at the Second International Congress for the Study of Child Language, Vancouver, B.C., August 1981.

Braunwald, Susan R., and Richard W. Brislin. The diary method updated. In E. Ochs and B. B. Schieffelin (Eds.), *Developmental Pragmatics*. New York: Academic Press, 1979.

Browman, Catherine P. Tip of the tongue and slip of the ear: implications for language processing. *UCLA Working Papers in Phonetics*, 1978, No. 42.

Brown, Roger. *A First Language: The Early Stages*. Cambridge, Mass.: Harvard University Press, 1973.

Brown, Roger, Courtney B. Cazden, and Ursula Bellugi. The child's grammar from I to III. In John P. Hill (Ed.), *Minnesota Symposium on Child Psychology* (Vol. 2). Minneapolis: University of Minnesota Press, 1969.

Brown, Roger, and Camille Hanlon. Derivational complexity and order of acquisition in child speech. In J. R. Hayes (Ed.), *Cognition and the Development of Language*. New York: John Wiley & Sons, 1970.

Bruner, Jerome S. The role of dialogue in language acquisition. In A. Sinclair, R. J. Jarvella, and W. J. M. Levelt (Eds.), *The Child's Conception of Language*. New York: Springer-Verlag, 1978.

Burling, Robbins. Language development of a Garo and English-speaking child. In Charles A. Ferguson and Dan I. Slobin (Eds.), *Studies of Child Language Development*. New York: Holt, Rinehart & Winston, 1973. (Reprinted from *Word*, 1959, *12*, 45–68.)

Cazden, Courtney B. Peekaboo as an instructional model: discourse development at home and at school. *Stanford Papers and Reports in Child Language Development*, 1979, *17*, 1–29.

Chi, Je G., Elizabeth C. Dooling, and Floyd H. Gilles. Left–right asymmetries of the temporal speech areas of the human fetus. *Archives of Neurology*, 1977, *34*, 346–8.

Clark, Herbert H., and Eve V. Clark. *Psychology and Language: An Introduction to Psychology and Linguistics*. New York: Harcourt Brace Jovanovich, 1977.

Clark, Ruth. Performing without competence. *Journal of Child Language*, 1974, *1*, 1–10.

Clark, Ruth. What's the use of imitation? *Journal of Child Language*, 1977, *4*, 341–58.

Crick, F. H. C. Thinking about the brain. *Scientific American*, 1979, No. 9, pp. 219–32.

Cross, Toni G. Mothers' speech adjustments: the contribution of selected child listener variables. In Catherine E. Snow and Charles A. Ferguson (Eds.), *Talking to Children: Language Input and Acquisition*. Cambridge: Cambridge University Press, 1977.

Dale, Philip S. *Language Development: Structure and Function* (2nd ed.). New York: Holt, Rinehart & Winston, 1976.

DeLoache, J., and A. Brown. Looking for Big Bird: studies of memory in very young children. *Quarterly Newsletter of the Laboratory of Comparative Human Cognition*, 1979, *1* (4), 53–7.

deVilliers, Peter and Jill deVilliers. *Language Acquisition*. Cambridge, Mass.: Harvard University Press, 1978.

Eisenberg, Ann R. Developments in displaced reference: language learning through routine. Paper presented at the Second International Conference on the Study of Child Language, Vancouver, B.C., August 1981.

Ekmeci, Ozden Fatma. Acquisition of Turkish. Doctoral dissertation, University of Texas at Austin, 1979. (University Microfilms No. 7928282)

Ewing, Guy. Word-order invariance and variability in five children's three-word utterances: a limited scope analysis. Paper presented at the Second International Congress for the Study of Child Language, Vancouver, B.C., August 1981.

Ferguson, Charles A. The structure and use of politeness formulas. *Language in Society*, 1976, *5*, 137–51.

Ferguson, Charles A. Baby talk as a simplified register. In Catherine E. Snow and Charles A. Ferguson (Eds.), *Talking to Children: Language Input and Acquisition*. Cambridge: Cambridge University Press, 1977.

Ferrier, Linda J. Some observations of error in context. In Natalie Waterson and Catherine Snow (Eds.), *The Development of Communication*. New York: John Wiley & Sons, 1978.

Fillmore, Charles J. On the organization of the semantic information in the lexicon. *Papers from the Parasession on the Lexicon*, Chicago Linguistic Society, 1978, pp. 148–73.

Fischer, Susan D., and Bonnie Gough. Verbs in American Sign Language. *Sign Language Studies*, 1978, *18*, 17–48.

Fraser, Bruce. Idioms within a transformational grammar. *Foundations of Language*, 1970, *4*(2), 109–27.

Fried, Itzhak, Peter E. Tanguay, Elena Boder, Catherine Doubleday, and Marcia Greensite. Developmental dyslexia: electrophysiological evidence of clinical subgroups. *Brain and Language*, 1981, *12*, 14–22.

Frishberg, Nancy. Arbitrariness and iconicity: historical changes in American Sign Language. *Language*, 1975, *51*, 696–719.

Fromkin, Victoria A. Appendix. In V. A. Fromkin (Ed.), *Speech Errors as Linguistic Evidence*. The Hague: Mouton, 1973.

Garnes, Sara, and Zinny S. Bond. A slip of the ear: a snip of the ear? a slip of the year? In Victoria A. Fromkin (Ed.), *Errors in Linguistic Performance: Slips of the Tongue, Ear, Pen, and Hand*. New York: Academic Press, 1980.

Garnica, Olga K. Some prosodic and paralinguistic features of speech to young children. In Catherine E. Snow and Charles A. Ferguson (Eds.), *Talking to Children: Language Input and Acquisition*. Cambridge: Cambridge University Press, 1977.

Geschwind, Norman. Some comments on the neurology of language. In David Caplan (Ed.), *Biological Studies of Mental Processes*. Cambridge, Mass.: MIT Press, 1980.

Gleason, Jean Berko, and Sandra Weintraub. The acquisition of routines in child language. *Language in Society*, 1976, *5*, 129–36.

Gleason, Jean Berko, and Sandra Weintraub. Input language and the acquisition of communicative competence. In Keith Nelson (Ed.), *Children's Language* (Vol. 1). New York: Gardner Press, 1978.

Grégoire, Antoine. L'Apprentissage du langage. In A. Bar-Adon and W. F. Leopold (Eds.), *Child Language: A Book of Readings*. Englewood Cliffs, N.J.: Prentice-Hall, 1971. (Excerpt translated and reprinted from *L'Apprentissage du Langage*, originally published, 1948.)

Guillaume, Paul. The development of formal elements in the child's speech. In Charles A. Ferguson and Dan I. Slobin (Eds.), *Studies of Child Language Development*. New York: Holt, Rinehart & Winston, 1973a. (Originally published, 1927.)

Guillaume, Paul. First stages of sentence formation in children's speech. In Charles A. Ferguson and Dan I. Slobin (Eds.), *Studies of Child Language Development*. New York: Holt, Rinehart & Winston, 1973b. (Originally published, 1927.)

Gumperz, John J., and Dell Hymes (Eds.). *Directions in Sociolinguistics: The Ethnography of Communication*. New York: Holt, Rinehart & Winston, 1972.

Hagen, John W., and Keith E. Stanovich. Memory: strategies of acquisition. In Robert V. Kail and John W. Hagen (Eds.), *Perspectives on the Development of Memory and Cognition*. New York: John Wiley & Sons, 1977.

Hakuta, Kenji. Prefabricated patterns and the emergence of structure in second language acquisition. *Language Learning*, 1974, *24*, 287–97.

Halliday, M. A. K. *Explorations in the Functions of Language*. London: Edward Arnold, 1973.

Halliday, M. A. K. *Learning How to Mean: Explorations in Development of Language*. New York: Elsevier, 1975.

Hatch, Evelyn. Some studies in language learning. *UCLA Workpapers in Teaching English as a Second Language*, 1972, *6*, 29–36.

Hayes-Roth, Barbara. Evolution of cognitive structures and processes. *Psychological Review*, 1977, *84*, 260–78.

Heath, Shirley Brice. Questioning at home and at school: a comparative study. In George Spindler (Ed.), *Doing the Ethnography of Schooling: Educational Anthropology in Action*. New York: Holt, Rinehart & Winston, 1982.

Heath, Shirley Brice. *Ways with Words: Language, Life and Work in Communities and Classrooms*. Cambridge: Cambridge University Press, 1983.

Horgan, Dianne. Nouns: love 'em or leave 'em. In V. Teller and S. J. White (Eds.), *Studies in Child Language and Multilingualism*. New York: Annals of the New York Academy of Sciences, 1980.

Huang, Joseph, and Evelyn Hatch. A Chinese child's acquisition of English. In Evelyn Hatch (Ed.), *Second Language Acquisition: A Book of Readings*. Rowley, Mass: Newbury House, 1978.

Huebner, Thomas. A longitudinal analysis of the interlanguage of an adult Hmong English learner. Doctoral dissertation, University of Hawaii, 1982.

Iwamura, Susan G. "I don' wanna don' throw": speech formulas in first language acquisition. Manuscript, University of Hawaii, 1979.

Iwamura, Susan Grohs. *The Verbal Games of Pre-school Children*. London: Croom Helm, 1980.

Jakobson, Roman. *Child Language, Aphasia and Phonological Universals*. The Hague: Mouton, 1968. (Originally published, 1941.)

Johnson, Carolyn E. The ontogenesis of question words in children's language. Paper presented at the Fifth Annual Boston University Conference on Language Development, October 1980.

Joos, Martin. *The Five Clocks*. New York: Harcourt, Brace & World, 1967.

Jordan, A. C. *A Practical Course in Xhosa*. Johannesburg: Longmans, 1966.

Kintsch, Walter. *Memory and Cognition* (2nd ed.). New York: John Wiley & Sons, 1977.

Krashen, Stephen. Some issues relating to the monitor model. In H. D. Brown, C. A. Yorio, and R. H. Crymes (Eds.), *On TESOL '77: Teaching and Learning English as a Second Language*. Washington, D.C.: Teachers of English to Speakers of Other Languages, 1977.

Krashen, Stephen. The Monitor model for second-language acquisition. In R. C. Gingras (Ed.), *Second Language Acquisition and Foreign Language Teaching*. Arlington, Va.: Center for Applied Linguistics, 1978.

Krashen, Stephen, and Robin Scarcella. On routines and patterns in language acquisition and performance. *Language Learning*, 1978, *28*, 283–300.

Kunene, Euphrasia Constantine Lwandle. The acquisition of SiSwati as a first language. Doctoral dissertation, University of California at Los Angeles, 1979. (University Microfilms No. 7926038)

Labov, William. *Language in the Inner City: Studies in Black English Vernacular*. Philadelphia: University of Pennsylvania Press, 1972.

Lamendella, John T. The neurofunctional basis of pattern practice. *TESOL Quarterly*, 1979, *13*, 5–19.

Lawler, Robert. Pre-readers' concepts of the English word. *MIT Artificial Intelligence Memo*, 1976, No. 395.

Leopold, Werner F. *Speech Development of a Bilingual Child: A Linguist's Record*. Volume 1, *Vocabulary Growth in the First Two Years*. Evanston, Ill.: Northwestern University Press, 1939.

Leopold, Werner. Patterning in children's language learning. In A. Bar-Adon and W. F. Leopold (Eds.), *Child Language: A Book of Readings*. Englewood Cliffs, N.J.: Prentice-Hall, 1971. (Reprinted from *Language Learning*, 1953, *5*.)

Lieven, Elena. Conversations between mothers and children: individual differences and their possible implication for the study of language learning. In Natalie Waterson and Catherine Snow (Eds.), *The Development of Communication*. New York: John Wiley & Sons, 1978.

Littlewood, William. *Communicative Language Teaching*. Cambridge: Cambridge University Press, 1981.

Macken, Marlys A. Developmental reorganization of phonology: a hierarchy of basic units of acquisition. *Lingua*, 1979, *49*, 11–49.

MacWhinney, Brian J. How Hungarian children learn to speak. Doctoral dissertation, University of California at Berkeley, 1974. (University Microfilms No. 74-11,777)

MacWhinney, Brian. Hungarian research on the acquisition of morphology and syntax. *Journal of Child Language*, 1976, *3*, 397–410.

MacWhinney, Brian. The acquisition of morphophonology. *Monographs of the Society for Research in Child Development*, 1978, *43*(1–2, Serial No. 174).

Miller, Peggy J. Amy, Wendy, and Beth: a study of early language development in South Baltimore. Doctoral dissertation, Columbia University, 1979.

Moerk, Ernst L., and Claudia Moerk. Quotations, imitations, and generalizations: factual and methodological analyses. *International Journal of Behavioral Development*, 1979, *2*, 43–72.

Montgomery, J. Anne. Sibling intervention in first language acquisition. Paper presented at the meeting of the Linguistic Society of America, Honolulu, July 1977.

Nagy, William. Some non-idiom larger-than-word units in the lexicon. *Papers from the Parasession on the Lexicon*, Chicago Linguistic Society, 1978, pp. 289–300.

Nelson, Katherine. Structure and strategy in learning to talk. *Monographs of the Society for Research in Child Development*, 1973, *39*(1–2, Serial No. 149).

Nelson, Katherine. Individual differences in language development: implications for development and language. *Developmental Psychology*, 1981, *17*, 170–87.

Newkirk, Don, Edward S. Klima, Carlene Canady Pedersen, and Ursula Bellugi. Linguistic evidence from slips of the hand. In Victoria A. Fromkin (Ed.), *Errors in Linguistic Performance: Slips of the Tongue, Ear, Pen, and Hand*. New York: Academic Press, 1980.

Newport, Elissa L. Constraints on structure: evidence from American Sign Language and language learning. In W. Andrew Collins (Ed.), *Minnesota Symposium on Child Psychology* (Vol. 14). Hillsdale, N.J.: Erlbaum, 1981.

Newport, Elissa L., Henry Gleitman, and Lila R. Gleitman. Mother, I'd rather do it myself: some effects and non-effects of maternal speech style. In Catherine E. Snow and Charles A. Ferguson (Eds.), *Talking to Children: Language Input and Acquisition*. Cambridge: Cambridge University Press, 1977.

Nida, Eugene A. *Morphology: The Descriptive Analysis of Words* (2nd ed.). Ann Arbor: University of Michigan Press, 1949.

Ninio, Anat, and Jerome Bruner. The achievements and antecedents of labelling. *Journal of Child Language*, 1978, *5*, 1–15.

Ochs, Elinor. Talking to children in Western Samoa. Manuscript, University of Southern California, 1980.

Olson, Gary M. Developmental changes in memory and the acquisition of language. In T. E. Moore (Ed.), *Cognitive Development and the Acquisition of Language*. New York: Academic Press, 1973.

Pawley, Andrew, and Frances Syder. Creativity vs. memorization in spontaneous discourse: the role of institutionalized sentences. Manuscript, University of Auckland, New Zealand, 1976.

Peters, Ann M. The beginnings of speech. *Stanford Papers and Reports in Child Language Development*, 1974, *8*, 26–32.

Peters, Ann M. Language learning strategies: does the whole equal the sum of the parts? *Language*, 1977, *53*, 560–73.

Peters, Ann M. The units of language acquisition. *University of Hawaii Working Papers in Linguistics*, 1980, *12*(1), 1–72.

Peters, Ann M. Language typology and the segmentation problem in early child language acquisition. *Proceedings of the Seventh Annual Meeting of the Berkeley Linguistics Society*, 1981, pp. 236–48.

Peters, Ann M., and Eran Zaidel. The acquisition of homonymy. *Cognition*, 1980, *8*, 187–207.

Phillips, Juliet R. Syntax and vocabulary of mothers' speech to young children: age and sex comparisons. *Child Development*, 1973, *44*, 182–5.

Poggi, Claudine. Imitation as a language learning strategy: evidence from a Chinese child. *Stanford Papers and Reports in Child Language Development*, 1982, *21*, 79–86.

Pye, Clifton. The acquisition of grammatical morphemes in Quiche Mayan. Doctoral dissertation, University of Pittsburgh, 1980.

Pye, Clifton. Mayan telegraphese: intonational determinants of inflectional development in Quiche Mayan. Paper given at the Second International Congress for the Study of Child Language, Vancouver, B.C., August 1981.

Ratner, Nancy, and Jerome S. Bruner. Games, social exchange and the acquisition of language. *Journal of Child Language*, 1978, *5*, 391–401.

Rosenberg, Sheldon. Semantic constraints on sentence production. In Sheldon Rosenberg (Ed.), *Sentence Production*. Hillsdale, N.J.: Erlbaum, 1977.

Sachs, Jacqueline. The adaptive significance of linguistic input to prelinguistic infants. In Catherine E. Snow and Charles A. Ferguson (Eds.), *Talking to Children: Language Input and Acquisition*. Cambridge: Cambridge University Press, 1977a.

Sachs, Jacqueline. Talking about the there and then. *Stanford Papers and Reports in Child Language Development*, 1977b, *13*, 56–63.

Sachs, Jacqueline, and Lynn Truswell. Comprehension of two-word instructions by children in the one-word stage. *Journal of Child Language*, 1978, *5*, 17–24.

Schieffelin, Bambi B. How Kaluli children learn what to say, what to do, and how to feel: an ethnographic study of the development of communicative competence. Doctoral dissertation, Columbia University, 1979.

Schieffelin, Bambi B., and Ann R. Eisenberg. Cultural variation in children's conversations. In Richard L. Schiefelbusch and Diane D. Bricker (Eds.), *Early Language: Acquisition and Intervention*. Baltimore: University Park Press, 1981.

Scollon, Ron. *Conversations with a One Year Old: A Case Study of the Developmental Foundation of Syntax*. Honolulu: University of Hawaii Press, 1976.

Shatz, Marilyn, and Rochel Gelman. Beyond syntax: the influence of conversational constraints on speech modifications. In Catherine E. Snow and Charles A. Ferguson (Eds.), *Talking to Children: Language Input and Acquisition*. Cambridge: Cambridge University Press, 1977.

Slobin, Dan I. Cognitive prerequisites for the development of grammar. In Charles A. Ferguson and Dan I. Slobin (Eds.), *Studies of Child Language Development*. New York: Holt, Rinehart & Winston, 1973.

Slobin, Dan I. Materials for the crosslinguistic study of language acquisition. Manuscript, University of California at Berkeley, 1981.

Slobin, Dan I., and Ayhan A. Aksu. Acquisition of Turkish. Manuscript, University of California at Berkeley, 1980.

Snow, Catherine E. The development of conversation between mothers and babies. *Journal of Child Language*, 1977, *4*, 1–22.

Snow, Catherine E. The uses of imitation. *Journal of Child Language*, 1981a, *8*, 205–12.

Snow, Catherine E. Saying it again: the role of expanded and deferred imitations in language acquisition. Manuscript, Harvard University, 1981b.

Snow, Catherine E., and Charles A. Ferguson, (Eds.). *Talking to Children: Language Input and Acquisition*. Cambridge: Cambridge University Press, 1977.

Stoel-Gammon, Carolyn, and Lenor Cabral. Learning how to tell it like it is: the development of the reportative function in children's speech. *Stanford Papers and Reports in Child Language Development*, 1977, *13*, 64–71.

Terrace, H. S., L. A. Petitto, R. J. Sanders, and T. G. Bever. Can an ape construct a sentence? *Science*, 1979, *206*, 891–906.

Thomas, Elizabeth K. It's all routine: a redefinition of routines as a central factor in language acquisition. Manuscript, Boston University, 1980.

Tolbert, Mary K. The Acquisition of Grammatical Morphemes: A Cross-Linguistic Study with Reference to Mayan (Cakchiquel) and Spanish. Doctoral dissertation, Harvard University, 1978.

van der Geest, Ton. Some interactional aspects of language acquisition. In Catherine E. Snow and Charles A. Ferguson (Eds.), *Talking to Children: Language Input and Acquisition*. Cambridge: Cambridge University Press, 1977.

van Lancker, Diana. Heterogeneity in language and speech: neurological studies. *UCLA Working Papers in Phonetics*, 1975, No. 29.

van Lancker, Diana, and Gerald J. Canter. Idiomatic versus literal interpretations of ditropically ambiguous sentences. *Journal of Speech and Hearing Research*, 1981, *24*, 64–9.

van Lancker, Diana, Gerald J. Canter, and Dale Terbeek. Disambiguation of ditropic sentences: acoustic and phonetic cues. *Journal of Speech and Hearing Research*, 1981, *24*, 330–5.

Vihman, Marilyn M. Formulas in first and second language acquisition. *Stanford Papers and Reports in Child Language Development*, 1979, *18*, 75–92.

Wada, J., R. Clarke, and A. Hamm. Cerebral hemispheric asymmetry in humans. *Archives of Neurology*, 1975, *32*, 239–46.

Weeks, Thelma E. *The Slow Speech Development of a Bright Child*. Lexington, Mass.: Lexington Books, 1974.

Weir, Ruth H. *Language in the Crib*. The Hague: Mouton, 1962.

Whitaker, Harry A. Automatization: a neurolinguistic model. Forum lecture, Linguistic Society of America Summer Institute, Salzburg, Austria, August 1979.

Whitaker, Harry A., and Ola A. Selnes. Anatomic variations in the cortex: individual differences and the problem of the localization of language functions. In S. R. Harnad, H. D. Steklis, and J. Lancaster (Eds.), *Origins and Evolution of Language and Speech*. New York: Annals of the New York Academy of Sciences, 1976.

Wickelgren, Wayne A. Chunking and consolidation: a theoretical synthesis of semantic networks, configuring in conditioning, S-R versus cognitive learning, normal forgetting, the amnesic syndrome, and the hippocampal arousal system. In John G. Seamon (Ed.), *Human Memory: Contemporary Readings*. New York: Oxford University Press, 1980.

Wilkins, David A. *Notional Syllabuses*. London: Oxford University Press, 1976.

Witelson, Sandra F., and Wazir Pallie. Left hemisphere specialization for language in the newborn. *Brain*, 1973, *96*, 641–6.

Wong Fillmore, Lily. The Second Time Around: Cognitive and Social Strategies in Second Language Acquisition. Doctoral dissertation, Stanford University, 1976.

Wong Fillmore, Lily. Individual differences in second language acquisition. In C. J. Fillmore, D. Kempler, and W. S-Y. Wang (Eds.), *Individual Differences in Language Ability and Language Behavior*. New York: Academic Press, 1979.

Wong Fillmore, Lily. Learning a second language: Chinese children in the American classroom. Paper presented at the Thirty-first Annual Georgetown University Roundtable on Languages and Linguistics, March 1980.

Author index

Akamatsu, C. T., x, 95, 105
Aksu, A. A., 20, 103
Anderson, J. R., 86

Barber, E. J. W., x, 5, 64, 87, 110
Bateson, M. C., 3, 6, 38, 80–1
Bauman, R., 29
Bellugi, U., 1, 107
Berko, J., 1 (*see also* Gleason, J. B.)
Berman, R. A., x, 27, 29, 37, 48, 103
Berthoud-Papandropolou, I., 101
Bisazza, J., x, 2–3, 64, 86, 90, 100
Bloom, L., 1, 5, 9, 17, 20, 28, 70
Bloomfield, L., 92
Blount, B. G., 29, 31–2
Boggs, S. T., x, 64
Bolinger, D., 2, 11, 40, 81, 90, 92
Bond, Z. S., 59–60, 64
Braine, M. D. S., 20, 42, 45–7, 53, 70
Branigan, G., 10
Braunwald, S. R., 28, 97
Brislin, R. W., 28, 97
Browman, C. P., 59–60, 64
Brown, A., 17
Brown, R., 1, 5, 7, 12, 15, 39–40, 70, 94–6,
      104, 111
Bruner, J. S., 29, 65–7, 99
Burling, R., 8, 13, 94, 104

Cabral, L., 69, 99
Canter, G. J., 108
Cazden, C. B., 1, 69, 99
Chi, J. G., 34
Clark, E. V., 42
Clark, H. H. and E. V., 5, 108
Clark, R., x, 5, 8–9, 11, 19, 27, 40, 47,
      73–8, 88, 111
Clarke, R., 34
Crick, F. H. C., 86
Cross, T. G., 23–4

Dale, P. S., 5
DeLoache, J., 17
deVilliers, P. and J., 5–6
Dooling, E. C., 34
Dorian, N., 107

Eisenberg, A. R., 29, 31–2, 69
Ekmeci, O. F., 20, 103
Ewing, G., 53

Ferguson, C. A., 2, 29, 112
Ferrier, L. J., 28
Fillmore, C. J., x, 64, 90, 106
Fischer, S. D., x, 78, 105
Fraser, B., 2
Fried, I. et al., 33
Frishberg, N., 81
Fromkin, V. A., 100, 106

Garnes, S., 59–60, 64
Garnica, O. K., 19, 23–4, 27, 61–2
Gelman, R., 23
Geschwind, N., 34
Gibson, R., 38
Gilles, F. H., 34
Gleason, J. B., 11, 28, 65, 99
Gleitman, H., 23
Gleitman, L. R., 23
Gough, B., 105
Gregoire, A., 102–3
Guillaume, P., 103, 107
Gumperz, J. J., 29

Hagen, J. W., 36
Hakuta, K., 13
Halliday, M. A. K., 6, 21, 101
Hamm, A., 34
Hanlon, C., 12, 14, 111
Hatch, E. M., 13, 111
Hayasaka, S., 51–2

Subject index

125